MONIQUE MAYS

I0081404

SELF-ESTEEM

Is The

NEW BLACK

How to become the confident woman

you have always wanted to be!

Editor: Laci Swann – Sharp Editorial, LLC

Cover design: Christy L. Staples – Get Launched

Cover photo: Jaio Photography

Formatting: Angela Shockley – That Formatting Lady

Scripture quotations are from the New American Standard Version Bible

DEDICATION

This book is dedicated to my seven daughters: Paris, Brooklynn, Destiny, Jada, Makiethia, Jordynn, and Darian. You are worthy, enough, and beautiful, just the way you are!

Love,
Mommy

CONTENTS

ACKNOWLEDGMENTS

First and foremost, all the glory and honor goes to my Lord and Savior Jesus Christ.

To my husband, Derrell, thank you for loving me along my journey in learning who I am. Thank you for seeing the beauty in me before I ever saw it in myself. I love you so much.

To my parents, I love you and thank you for all you have done for me.

To my Granppy, thank you for the wisdom you have given me and the lessons you have taught me to become the woman I am today.

Thank you to my best friend, Lakisha, for being my ear and my anchor, and, most of all, thank you for being there through everything!

A very special thank you to my family and friends for their encouragement, love, and support. You are truly appreciated!

INTRODUCTION

"Ma'am, we can see you! Come out of the bushes!" the officer shouted from his police car.

"Okay," I meekly said as I pulled myself to my feet.

"Do you know what time it is?" the officer asked.

"Yes, sir, I do," I replied, looking down at my feet, trying not to let my nerves show.

"We received a call from the gas station owner down the road," he sternly continued. "The owner said he saw a young girl in a bright yellow jacket, and a male, walking down the street in the dark. He was concerned. And why are you hiding behind the bushes?" he asked, trying to hold back his laughter.

"Well, sir... I was scared," I whispered.

"Okay, well, we will call your parents and let them know

you are okay," he stated.

"No, no! Please don't do that! Can I please finish walking home? I'm almost there," I pleaded.

Instead, the officer offered to take me home, and I accepted. I was sitting in the back of the cold police car feeling absolutely petrified. Thoughts began racing through my mind.

What if my mom is awake?

What if someone notices me getting out of the squad car?

Why in the world was I trying to hide behind a bush, wearing a highlighter-bright jacket, anyway?!

As we pulled up to my duplex, the officer looked back at me and sternly said, "I'm going to let you go this time. Don't let it happen again!"

"Thank you, sir!" I excitedly said, thanking him for my lucky break.

I jumped out of the car and quietly crawled back into the window I had snuck out of. I spent the rest of the night in my bed, hoping the officer would not come back and tell my mother where I was or what I did. I had it bad, and it was just the beginning...

***

At the time of that incident, I was truly confused, a lost teenager. Now, as a grown woman, I am able to clearly see that. I have since evolved into a confident individual, secure in who I am and firm in my standards, a far cry from the young, impressionable girl in the bright yellow jacket. As a wife, proud mother, women's ministry teacher, and successful motivational speaker, I want to share how to effectively strengthen your self-esteem through establishing standards and boundaries as well as guiding you to fully loving yourself, flaws and all. The best teacher is life experience, and I have many. I would like to share my experiences with you in hopes you can see there is a way out.

***

Why do women have such a hard time acquiring and maintaining self-confidence? Women are often taught and encouraged to take care of others before taking care of themselves, and thinking too highly of ourselves is deemed selfish. By nature, women are nurturers, and nurturing qualities are ingrained in our inner-most being. Somewhere along the way, we have forgotten how to give that same, nurturing love to ourselves – to care for ourselves, forgive ourselves, and require that the people we come in contact with treat us in the manner in which we deserve to be treated. In the coming pages, you will discover the steps to take to become the confident woman you always wanted to be. This book will encourage you to use the innate wisdom you have always possessed, but possibly ignored, or have yet to uncover.

Self-Esteem Is the New Black is not your average self-help book. This book is more than guidance and instruction on a page. *Self-Esteem Is the New Black* provides knowledge and faith-based insight while encouraging each reader to take their journey, two steps further, through practical application. You will not only be given information on how to boost your self-esteem, but you will be given the tools to acknowledge and exude strong, genuine feelings of self-love. Self-esteem coupled with self-love is a recipe for success, happiness, and contentment, which will inevitably shine in your life, personally and professionally. I share my mistakes and struggles in hopes of showing you that you can overcome yours as well. My goal is to not only share how to become the confident woman you have always wanted to be, but to show you through self-reflective exercises how to achieve the life you deserve. What is information if you have no application, right? *Right!* At the end of each chapter, you will find one exercise and one affirmation. *Try It on for Size* is the practical step you need to accomplish what is explained in the respective chapter. Take your time, and thoroughly complete the exercise. Do not rush. Completing each exercise is precisely where your wisdom will begin to form and grow. Some exercises are brief while other exercises will take you weeks to complete. The same way you try on different outfits in the dressing room, you must keep trying these exercises on for size until you get the perfect fit – a well-rounded, established sense of self-esteem. *Mirror Work* is an affirmation to say aloud. Your mind believes no other voice more than your own. So, continuously speak the affirmations as you work through the book. Recite, recite, recite. Think of this book as your guide to attaining unwavering confidence. To get the most out of this book, I encourage you to read the chapters, one page at a time, and work on each specific area until you are emotionally and mentally ready to proceed. You must thoughtfully apply yourself with each and every word. Do your exercises and speak your affirmations. The confident woman you have always wanted to be is waiting for you on the other end of this book!

The time has come to get back to the basics. Loving yourself is a must-have, like the little black dress that remains a classic staple in your closet. *Self-esteem IS the new black*! So, are you ready for a change? Let's work!

I – FORGIVENESS

"When you forgive, you in no way change the past – but you sure do change the future." – Bernard Meltzer

What shapes the opinions you have of yourself?

When you are born into the world, you arrive without a care in the world, innocent and wide-eyed. As time progresses, and various influences come in and out of your life, you begin to form opinions – opinions of yourself, opinions about others, and opinions about the world. Typically, experiences shape opinions. More profoundly, what other people have told you about yourself shapes your thoughts and feelings, especially regarding who you are. This truth can go one of two ways – you can be uplifted by kind, encouraging, gracious opinions or you can be scarred by damaging words. It is safe to assume every last one of us has experienced both, the enriching opinions and the demeaning, harsh judgements. The truth is, no one is exempt from judgement or criticism. Not a soul on Earth. After all, Jesus was denied, judged, doubted, disowned, and talked badly about:

And He came home, and the crowd gathered again, to such an extent that they could not even eat a meal. When His own people heard of this, they went out to take custody of Him; for they were saying, "He has lost His senses" (Mark 3: 20-21).

So, if people talked about Jesus, what makes you think no one would talk about you? Sadly, some opinions and judgements permeate our souls in a way that never seem to escape our minds. They become embedded in our minds to the point of embodying these judgements, which are all too often demeaning, degrading, and completely off the mark.

Can you think back to a specific time when someone said something to you that hurt you to your core? A comment so scarring that the words have yet to escape your mind? I know I can. In fact, I remember one particular memory all too well...

I was pregnant at the young age of 16, a teen mom who went from enjoying typical high school days to late night feedings. At that time, several adults in my life hardly held back their opinions about my teenage pregnancy. Truth be told, I was constantly told how stupid I was and that I ruined my life. While I made an adult-like decision with my child's father, which inevitably led to my pregnancy, I still had the mind of a 16 year old, yet my feelings were not spared, whatsoever, by the adults in my life.

"How could you do this, Monique?!" they demanded.

"You had your whole life ahead of you!" they yelled.

"How stupid could you be?" I was heartlessly asked.

Despite the harsh words, constant badgering, and insensitive line of questioning, I was not exactly sure they were wrong about me or my situation. While I was bombarded with the unwanted opinions of others, I made the decision that their words held no power over my destiny. Nevertheless, the questions and comments had an effect on my self-esteem. After all, I was human. Furthermore, I was a sensitive, impressionable teenager, and although my confidence carried me through, there were times I stumbled and took a few steps back. As time progressed, I began to question myself, my worth, and my intelligence, or lack thereof.

"You made the honor roll, Monique! You were on the track team and you made the dance team, too. How did this happen?! What were you thinking? Why did you let this happen?" I would continuously ask myself.

In retrospect, my self-badgering was more emotionally detrimental than the harsh words from other adults and peers. Remember, your voice will always resonate more profoundly than any other voice. Despite my repetitive line of questioning and constant retrospection, I knew exactly how this teenage pregnancy came to happen. Well, besides the obvious "birds and bees" explanation. In hindsight, I became pregnant at a young age for reasons far deeper than physically connecting with someone else.

During my childhood years, I was an army brat, so I moved around quite a bit. Born on a military base in Germany, I did not come to America until I was about two years old. Washington, California, Nevada, Florida, Tennessee, Pennsylvania, and Kentucky have all been my home, at one point, as a child. One downfall about living in so many places is that I did not have a sense of consistency. My life was different and ever-changing in each place, experiencing constant change, new environments, and new groups of people, too. In some places, I was embraced and treated kindly. In other places, not so much, not so much at all. This refusal and inconsistency left a desire in my heart to be both settled and attached. Wanting to be settled in one place is perfectly fine, but longing for physical attachment is where my self-esteem problems developed.

After years of moving here and there, our family became semi-settled during my high school years, and there I discovered a new type of attention – attention from the opposite sex! I was intrigued by this new feeling of being wanted by a male. The feeling of receiving attention in the hallways, and getting phone calls at home, made me feel important. I flirted, and boys reciprocated. I liked that. I thought I could get attention from whoever I wanted, and this newfound interest made me feel powerful, so powerful that I became prideful, too. The Bible tells us that pride comes before a fall: "Pride goes before destruction, a haughty spirit before a fall" (Proverbs 16:18). Well, I was no exception to experiencing a fall, and my destruction during my teenage years was rooted in my desire for attention.

There happened to be a young man on the same school bus who I began to like. The catch, though, was that he did not like me.

"How could this be?" I thought.

"Maybe he is just too shy to tell me," I told myself.

At the time, I was convinced I was the hottest thing around. Plus, I always had a bit of fight in me. If someone told me I could not do something, I was determined to prove that person wrong, and this situation was no different. However, hindsight is always 20/20. Looking back, I should have accepted his disinterest and moved forward, but I choose to take his inattention on as a challenge.

"I would make him like me!" I foolishly decided.

I was operating with a prideful mindset, unable to see that my downfall was sure to come. Nevertheless, I was a know-it-all teenager, completely unaware of how this situation would manifest. What started out as a seemingly harmless cat-and-mouse game turned into an adult situation.

I was a young girl dealing with a teenage boy, so he was hardly impressed by my intelligence. After all, most teenage boys do not want to talk about what we recently learned in class or topics circulating the news. Instead, I used what I knew would work – my body. I decided I would use my appearance to capture his attention. Initially, I thought this was a fun challenge. The game of cat and mouse was exciting and entertaining. So, I would walk with him to his parents' apartment, when we got off the bus, and hang out in his room. I went as far as crying, telling him how much I wanted to be with him. I would push myself on him, any chance I got, in hopes I would get the response I wanted – his affection and attention. I soon did.

"You did it, Monique. You got the boy!" I secretly applauded myself. "Mission accomplished," I thought.

As time went on, I became more and more attached to the feeling of someone wanting me. I was not used to consistency, and that was what I thought I was getting from this guy through our physical relationship. We soon became inseparable. All of those times I walked with him to his house after school turned into a regular, daily routine. I basically lived at his apartment. After a few months, my mother and I moved to the other side of town, but that did not stop me from spending time with him. I would sneak out of the house, and we would walk to meet each other. At this point, the challenge was no longer cat and mouse – we were both seeking each other's attention. One particular night, I decided to sneak out again, but this time I got caught. My mother discovered my laundry basket that was supposed to be blocking my bedroom door. To say she was livid was an understatement. As my boyfriend and I sat together in his room, the phone rang.

"Is Monique over there?!" my mother shouted through the

other end of the phone.

I was busted!

I ran out to my car and drove home, trying to think of the best excuse possible. The best excuse my teenage mind came up with was that I went for a drive. Not the best excuse, I know. Plus, my mother was "not born yesterday." She was hip to teenage games, and my game did not work on her. Needless to say, my mother did not believe my excuse. She did not entertain it for a second.

"I'm not going to have this in my house," she sternly said.

My mom decided to send me to live with my sister for the holiday break, in hopes I would get my mind back on track and off of this guy... though it was a little too late for that. My boy-friend and I spent every moment on the phone, planning the life we would have – how we would get married and a build a great life together. We would talk for hours and hours at a time. In fact, we talked any moment I could spare, and his mother was hardly pleased when she received her exorbitant phone bill. I was fool-ishly excited about the prospect of forever with my crush turned relationship. I realize, now, that I quickly attached my heart and mind to a dream and not a reality. I was attached to the idea of forever, especially since I was craving stability and attachment for the majority of my young life. I was wooed by words and head over heels for a dream. I convinced my mother that I would never sneak out again, with my fingers crossed behind my back, and I told her I wanted to come home. She agreed. When I arrived back home, he and I picked up where we left off, seeing each other every chance we could. A few months before I found out I was pregnant, my cycle was late. I was certain I was pregnant, but the test came out negative. Strangely, I felt a sense of loss for something I never had. When I expressed my feelings to him about my negative pregnancy test, he reassured me we would one day have a baby and get married, the fairy tale many young girls are told. Hearing those words made me feel lucky and loved, that I would have a baby and a family. I thought his words were more than promises because he expressed so much excitement about wanting a family with me, too. Nevertheless, my impressionable teenage mind was guiding me down a path that was anything but stable, which is what I craved in the first place. Through my choices, I received the attention I was so badly seeking, which caused me to make decisions I knew were not right or sound. I had no business sneaking out of my mother's house or having sex at such a young age. I did not think my decisions through. Instead, I acted impulsively in the moment and decided to deal with the consequences, if any, at a later time. I made adult-like choices knowing I could end up in hot water. And, well, hot water was what I found. I did not think past my emotions and took no precautions to prevent pregnancy. Not too long after we started having sex, I became pregnant. I was pregnant at sixteen, yet I was acting as if I was an adult, able to care and provide for a baby. I was so wrapped up in the idea of having a family that I forgot that I was still in high school, and a child was not some sort of baby doll. A child comes with great responsibility and significant costs, too – continual bills, doctor appointments, baby sitters, diapers, clothes, food, and much more. However, my mind was merely fixated on the joy of having a family of my own – the stability I thought I needed. Always remember – attention does not come free. The attention I was desperately seeking definitely came with a price. And sometimes, that price is higher than you would ever want to pay or you could ever afford.

While my current self is deep in faith with the knowledge and wisdom to make solid decisions, dedicating my life to Christ did not come until later in my life. So, I did not navigate through my teenage years making wise, faith-based choices. Instead, I made my way without His guidance. I was facing moral choices without biblical principals or an understanding of what direction I should face from God:

> I call heaven and earth to witness against you today, that I have set before you life and death, the blessing and the curse. So choose life in order that you may live, you and your descendants, by loving the Lord your God, by obeying His voice, and by holding fast to Him; for this is your life and the length of your days, that you may live in the land which the Lord swore to your fathers, to Abraham, Isaac, and Jacob, to give them (Deuteronomy 30: 19–20).

In October of my junior year of high school, something physically, did not feel right. Even at the young age of sixteen, I knew my body, and my body certainly did not feel the same. I had been throwing up and not feeling my best, experiencing dizziness, extreme fatigue, and nausea. I decided I would take a pregnancy test in the restroom of my job. My boyfriend stood outside of the bathroom door, patiently waiting for the news of one line or two. Well, two lines appeared, bright and clear. I was having a baby, and I was thrilled!

Before I came out of the stall, my boyfriend anxiously asked, "What does it say?"

"I'm pregnant!" I joyfully replied.

Sheer panic filled his face, and his response caught me completely off guard.

"Aren't you happy?" I confusedly asked.

As the words left my mouth, it was as if some sort of switch clicked in his mind. He smiled and said, "Of course!" I felt relieved, and, for a moment, the excitement of our secret filled me with joy, although it did not take long for the excitement to fade and reality to set in... I knew I had to tell my mother, and the mere thought made my pregnancy nausea feel like a casual stroll in the park. I was not ready to have a conversation with her about my pregnancy, not ready at all. The next day, however, I built up enough courage to break the news to her. After all, this was a secret I knew I could not hide for long.

As we sat together on the couch, I turned to her, and in a

frail, quiet tone I said, "Momma, I have something to tell you."

She glared at me and quickly asked, "You aren't pregnant, are you?"

Mothers have superpowers. They just *know*. A mother's intuition is sharper than a veteran detective on the job. Maybe my mom assumed I was pregnant based on the times she caught me sneaking out the house, I'm not sure. Or, she just knew for the reason moms know everything – the innate superpower all women have: gut instinct. Rarely does one's gut instinct fail. Few and far between do people confuse anxiety or paranoia with a strong gut feeling. This time, however, my mom was neither anxious nor paranoid. *She just knew.*

I held my head down and answered, "Yes, mom, I'm pregnant..."

Those few words were all I could muster the courage to say. I expected my mom to fly off the handle. I was expecting a lecture, some shouting, and the inevitable "I'm so disappointed" speech. Instead, I was greeted with the worst response I could have received at the time – silence, dead silence, the kind of silence that you can hear a pin drop in.

My mother did not speak to me for two days, and those two days felt like an eternity. She did not say a thing, not a single word. Although my mom and I were not incredibly close, enduring two days of silence was certainly out of the ordinary. Her silence put me in a tailspin as I anxiously waited for a blow up to eventually occur. I did not know what to do, but I knew I had royally messed up. I was accustomed to being in trouble if I brought home a "C" on my report card, and this situation was far worse than a mere "C" on a report card. When my mom finally talked to me, she sat me down in the living room and explained how disappointed she was. And so it began... the disappointment talk, the talk I was dreading. I hated letting down the people I cared about.

My mom screamed, "Why would you destroy your life?! That's your baby, and you are going to take care of this baby, not me!"

She made her thoughts very clear, shouting, over and over again, that she will not play mother to my child; this was my responsibility, not hers. Her next move caught me by surprise.

"Call your dad," she flatly instructed.

My dad was living in another state, so I felt a bit braver sharing the news over the phone instead of in person. I made the phone call and did not know what to expect. In my immature frame of mine, I thought my dad would understand. I thought, maybe, he would not explode. And maybe, just maybe, he would be okay with my news.

"I was daddy's girl, after all," I tried to convince myself.

"He would handle the news better than my mom," I assumed.

"This will be okay," I told myself as I waited for him to answer.

He picked up and joyfully said, "Hey, baby!"

Within a matter of seconds, my mother began yelling in

the background, "Tell him what you did, Monique! Tell him!" There was no turning back at this point. So, I built up all the courage I possibly could and said, "Daddy, I'm pregnant."

Again, the sound I grew to hate, silence, flooded the phone line.

"What?!" he loudly exclaimed. "How could you be so stupid?! "You were supposed to be the smart one, Monique!" my dad shouted in a rage.

I did not dare speak a word back. Defending myself was out of the question. I was afraid that if I gave a response it would only make the situation worse. I was ashamed. I was always the apple of my father's eye. In those few words he spoke, I felt that I had become an apple, alright – a rotten one. My dad then said, "I just can't believe this. I will call you back when I get over this."

I did not receive another call from my father until my daughter was born.

Despite the disappointment and disapproval of those closest to me, I decided to keep the baby. I nixed the options of abortion or adoption, choosing to move forward as a teenage mom. As I walked through the halls at school, with my stomach noticeably poking out, I was determined to prove everyone wrong. Sure, the stigma of teenage motherhood filled the minds of my peers, but I convinced myself that I knew exactly what I was doing and I could handle this situation.

I would graduate.

I would birth a healthy baby.

I would have a family.

I would be a great mom.

My life was not destroyed.

I tried to convince myself this situation would pan out. I knew I did not make the smartest choice by having sex at a young age, but I also knew I was still an intelligent young lady fully capable of graduating. A baby did not negate my intelligence or my ability to excel. I encouraged myself to earn great grades and attend every class, despite my bouts of morning sickness. I thought to myself, "I can still graduate, I can get a job, and this will work out." I quickly discovered that not only were those closest to me disappointed, but several others formed opinions about my pregnancy as well.

Do not be surprised when your struggle becomes a source of conversation. What may be a painful, challenging situation for you to navigate through may be an entertaining situation and conversation starter to another. However, being pregnant at such a young age was anything but entertaining. There I was, a high school teenager, barely at the age to drive, trying to get to the school bus on time after a session of morning sickness, then having to rush out of class because I had a baby resting on my bladder. Hardly entertaining! Nevertheless, there was no turning back. I owned up to my situation, and I was about to bring new life into this world.

Parents of my fellow classmates warned their daughters to stay away from me, "that type of girl", as they feared I would negatively influence their child. I was treated as though my pregnancy was contagious, a condition others would catch if they spent time with me. When school began the following year, my classmates were more than happy to report to me what was said about me before school let out. Sadly, and strangely, some of my classmates felt joy in gossiping to me about me. Apparently, the music teacher at school told her class I would never graduate. As an impressionable, sensitive seventeen-year-old young lady, those words devastated my soul. Even worse, those opinions held the power to determine how I felt about myself forever. Words are powerful... if you choose to take them in. I choose to take them in, but as fuel to propel my motivation. My journey of overcoming the harsh opinions of others did not begin in high school, actually. I had been dealing with the harsh opinions of others since elementary school.

Diving back into my memory bank, opinions I heard during my childhood boldly stand out in my mind. I was ruthlessly picked on in elementary school for being biracial. What is now seen as beautiful or exotic was definitely not the case in rural Kentucky in the 90's. I was not black enough for my black classmates nor white enough for my white classmates. I was a yellow-toned girl with bushy hair, often called "half-breed" or "zebra" and "mellow yellow." I would laugh along with whoever was calling me names, determined to not allow the hurt to show, when, in fact, I was upset. Deeply hurting, actually. Truth be told, I was devastated by the name-calling and laughter. After all, I was a little girl, certainly not emotionally equipped to deal with this level of torment and constant teasing. My classmates were laughing at me, certainly not with me. Children can be cruel, as we all know. However, one day, I made the bold, brave decision, during my walk home from the bus stop, to accept that those mean kids did not know who I truly was. I was beautiful to me. As I look back on that moment, embedded in my mind as clear as day, I give all the credit and glory to God because there was no way my little mind could have come up with that confident decision on my own. After that walk home from the bus stop, the fire I discussed earlier was officially lit. Once I made up my mind, that I was beautiful in my own right, the name-calling hurt less and less. I discovered an inward toughness, and I was not going to let the teasing and name-calling bother me anymore. Soon enough, believe it or not, the name-calling stopped. No more sneers and laughter. No more hearing "mellow yellow" or "zebra" when the teacher was no longer within earshot.

If someone discovers that their words are not getting a rise out of you anymore, they will stop. Not my circus, not my monkeys, right? I would not allow the words of others to cause me to question who I was. But because my newfound confidence was left unguided, it made me arrogant. There is a grave difference between confidence and arrogance, but I had yet to learn that lesson.

I could have taken those hurtful words and let them define me, but I chose otherwise. Their cruel words made me stronger, and my determination only grew fiercer. I was my own person! My classmates did not need to like me. I liked me! I did not know this at the time, but I was building self-confidence based on positive, loving feelings I had for myself and not the degrading opinions of others.

Did those words hurt?

Yes, of course.

Did letting go of those words take time?

Definitely.

There is a saying – "Sticks and stones may break my bones but words will never hurt me." I don't know who came up with that saying, but that is a flat out lie. Words hurt as much as sticks and stones. Actually, I would rather be hit by a stick or stone than hear an earful of cruel comments. Many of us have been hurt by others through words or actions. We often bury those words, deep inside of our souls, and each time we look in the mirror, those words rise up and we cannot seem to figure out why we are reveling in the negative opinions others have of us. So, how do you overcome those words to keep them from destroying your self-esteem?

You forgive and let go.

We extend forgiveness, even when an apology is not offered.

We choose to forgive, not for others, but for ourselves and our peace of mind.

We forgive because that is what Christ has called us to do

– show grace and forgiveness the way He continually forgives us: "In everything, therefore, treat people the same way you want them to treat you, for this is the Law of the Prophets" (Matthew 7:12). Many times, my words, actions, and decisions have disappointed God because they went against His Word, but He never threw in the towel on me. Instead, He gave me another chance. Chance after chance, actually.

His grace, unending.

His forgiveness, everlasting.

The scripture says forgive seventy times seven. Basically, He was directing us to forgive in an unlimited capacity. "Jesus said to him, 'I do not say to you, up to seven times, but up to seventy times seven'" (Matthew 18:22). Nevertheless, you must refuse to hold on to hurt, anger, resentment, or bitterness because those emotions will only cause you more pain, pushing you further from the person God wants you to be. As women of God, we are to emulate Christ, and if we are going to be like Jesus, we have to begin with His ultimate reason for coming which was to die for the sins of the world, offering us a channel to forgiveness.

When someone hurts you, and you choose to not forgive, you not only go against His Word, but you give that person power over your life. You give that person total control over your emotions, so much so that they have the power to control how you think of yourself even when they are not in your presence. You begin to think about the hurt they caused you, fixating on each word of every insult or unkind opinion. Those thoughts manifest into negative feelings, and those negative feelings permeate your mind. That string of destructive thinking offers power to those who hurt you. By holding on to their words, you are choosing to lose sight of who you truly are. More importantly, you are certainly not defined by their lesser-than opinions of you. You were fearfully and wonderfully made, not created to drown in sorrow and self-doubt. Understandably, there are times it's difficult to admit that you have been hurt or wronged, because revisiting the hurt often intensifies the pain, but through acknowledgement and forgiveness, you will find a place of healing.

If I would have chosen to digest the opinions of others during those formidable high school years, I would have stayed where I was – trapped by the negative opinions of others, convinced my life was ruined and I would never amount to anything. Worse, if I chose to allow the cruel opinions of my elementary school classmates to mold my self-esteem, I would have been an absolute mess in the following years – reveling in self-hate, refusing to accept my true self, unable to do anything unless I was receiving positive attention from people who never planned on reciprocating positivity anyway. Instead, I used those hurtful, doubtful, heartless words as fuel and propelled myself to continue my education.

The summer before my senior year, I gave birth to my daughter. One look in her adorable, innocent eyes and I knew I had to finish what I had started. I brought a new, pure life into this world, and I did not want to let her down. I approached my senior year determined to graduate so I could provide for my daughter the way she deserved. This is when reality set in for me. As the first week of my senior year approached, I received a phone call that I was not expecting.

"Hello, Monique?" I heard on the other line. "Umm, I don't want to do this anymore," he continued.

In total shock, I confusedly asked, "What don't you want to do anymore?"

He got straight to the point "Yeah, this just isn't fun anymore. I don't want to be with you."

Click.

My heart was in the pit of my stomach. I held the phone to my ear for what seemed like hours, trying to process what just happened, although he had hung up long before. Devastation could not compare to the actual emotion I felt in that moment. I was crushed. Heartbroken. Shocked. Betrayed. Furious!

"What about our family?!" I angrily wondered. "How could he just leave?" I thought.

At the time, he was a man I respected and loved. He was the person I trusted with my body and my future. In retrospect, of course, I was a smitten teenager, completely wooed by puppy love. I found my safety, happiness, and future in him, which was my greatest mistake. *Never allow yourself to be in total awe of a person. People will disappoint you, especially if you put those people in a place they never were meant to be in.* Any person or object receiving a higher priority and position than God, consuming the devotion you should be doing for the Lord, will be destined for disaster. More importantly, the only awe we should feel is toward our mighty God:

> Then God spoke all these words, saying, "I am the Lord your God, who brought you out of the land of Egypt, out of the house of slavery. You shall have no other gods before Me. You shall not make for yourself an idol, or any likeness of what is in heaven above or on the earth beneath or in the water under the earth. You shall not worship them or serve them; for I, the Lord your God, am a jealous God, visiting the iniquity of the fashions on the children, on the third and the fourth generations of those who hate Me, but showing lovingkindness to thousands, to those who love Me and keep My commandments" (Exodus 20:1-6).

He wants our time and attention, yet I was giving my time and attention to a young man who, initially, did not want anything to do with me. There I was, heartbroken, about to embark on the journey of single motherhood at the young age of seventeen. Just like that, the bubble I put myself in was burst. I was on my own. The fairy tale I was so sure of turned to a harsh reality. I took a few days to sulk, but I did not have much time to sit around and cry. The time had come to go back to school. I was scared and unsure of how single motherhood would unfold. Nevertheless, I could not stop, so I went back to school and pressed forward as diligently as possible. I found a sweet, trustworthy woman in my former apartment complex to watch my daughter during the day. I would pick my baby up in the afternoon, followed by an evening of housework and homework. Late at night, trying to write a thesis, and not wake my baby up, was challenging. I needed any amount of sleep I could get. Some afternoons, when I was off of work, I would pull out my books to try and get ahead. Although my teenage years are long gone, I reflect on this as if it were yesterday – my daughter crawling all over my books as I studied. Luckily, my school had a program which allowed students to leave halfway through the day, only if you had a job and enough credit hours. Thankfully, I had a job in fast food restaurant, so I went to school for half of the day and I cared for my baby and worked the remaining half. Despite my heartache, I had a plan, and I was ready to work my plans to the point of fruition. I was ready to finish high school on a positive note.

As my classmates and I sat in the stadium for graduation practice, a few faculty members began sharing class rankings with the students. My last name began with a "Y", so I knew I was last in line. They began to call the names for the honor graduate group because those students were allowed to walk across the field first. "V", "W", and "X" and then "Y".

"Monique York," a teacher announced.

There it was, my name! And no, my name was not called

in error. Me, Monique! My name was called, loud and clear!

The teen mom.

The underestimated.

The counted out.

The problem child.

I did it! I was an honor graduate!

The same teenage girl who was greeted in the hallways with sneers and whispers.

The same girl who was counted out by family and "friends" alike.

The same girl who was told her life was forever ruined.

Although I did not have a relationship with God at that time, I know He is the reason I made it through one of the most trying times in my life.

In that moment, while we were supposed to be focused on following instructions regarding graduation procedure, I could not help but zone out and reflect on how I got to that moment. I reflected on all the nights I studied until I could barely see straight, how I worked late nights and afterschool, how challenging it was to find a trustworthy babysitter, being kicked out the house and brought back in, and several other obstacles I battled. I experienced a great deal in such a short period of time, yet I overcame, and I was proud of myself. I mustered up every bit of restraint I had to not burst into tears. Happy tears. Tears of relief and joy. I was not who they said I was. I was the person I wanted to be, despite the doubts. In that moment, I realized that it was not about what others said that mattered; what mattered was what I said about me. My thoughts made a difference. I would soon learn that how God views me is of the utmost importance. He will forever see me as worthy of happiness, peace, and prosperity because that is how He purposefully made me to be: "But the very hairs of your head are all numbered" (Matthew 10:30). God crowned you with glory and honor, and we are saved by grace, justified by faith, and forever secure in His name. Never forget it!

More than the motivation to succeed, my extension of forgiveness proved far more powerful in my ability to progress beyond the opinions people boxed me into. My ability to forgive thwarted my success. My focus shifted from feeling angry and bitter towards those who hurt me to redirecting my feelings into positive energy. I was able to emotionally feed myself the moment I let go of their hurtful words. If you want to be the confident woman you always wanted to be, forgive the harsh, doubting words and negative actions of others. Free yourself from who they say you are, and walk into the woman you know you are!

Like my choir teacher in high school who doubted my ability to graduate, and the kids on the bus during my elementary school days, their words and actions had more to do with *them* than with *me*. The way others treat you is a direct reflection of the way they love themselves. A person rich in self-love will share words of love and kindness. And, if they do not have anything nice to say, they will not say anything at all. That is how a highly-esteemed person treats others – with grace and kindness, free of judgement. You cannot expect love from a person who does not love him or herself. When you recognize that the words and actions of individuals reflect their souls, and their capacity to love and forgive others, you will be able to see yourself more clearly. My Granppy once said, "If you look deep enough at a person who has hurt you, you can find a reason to feel sorry for them." Granppy is a wise man.

Did the kids on my school bus know they were being bullies, hurting me with their words?

Maybe.

Were those kids unsure of themselves and their looks, which is why they chose to make fun of the way I looked?

Quite possibly.

Or did those children come from homes that did not teach or expose them to biracial children and other cultures?

That could be a possibility, too.

I had to let their hurtful words go, regardless of the reasons behind their cruel behavior. In retrospect, they were children who were trying to find their identities, too.

What about the parents of my high school classmates, the parents who were afraid I would be a bad example to their daughters and sons? Now, as a mother, I can somewhat understand why those parents felt the way they did about my teenage pregnancy. The truth is, we want to make sure our children's friends are making wise choices. When teenagers make decisions we would not want for our own children, we, as parents, encourage our kids to steer clear.

In the case of my parents and their reactions to my news, I now understand their responses to my pregnancy announcement. They were shocked and disappointed. Understandably so. Who doesn't want the best for their child? I thank God that we have a great relationship now, and I thank my mother for giving me total responsibility of my choice. She meant what she said when she told me I would be raising my child. I did not dump my child on my parents, and I did not assume my parents would take on the role I should be playing. My mother's firm decision made me responsible; it made me a better mother. As for my dad, I'm daddy's girl once again. We have since had many conversations about that time and have moved past the unspoken feelings and initial reactions. Once my daughter was born, he fell head over heels for her. All is forgiven, and he is a great "Papa" to all of his granddaughters.

Now that I can clearly reflect on my first pregnancy, sans anger or resentment, I decided, "Why hold on to the anger or hurt of those comments?" I had to release those destructive feelings. No matter the reasons behind those cruel remarks, I chose to believe the reasons behind their cruelty no longer mattered. What I do know is that in order for me to be whole, I had to forgive. I had to release each person who hurt me from being hostage in my heart because holding on was not hurting them. Holding on was not punishing them, either. And holding on was not teaching them a lesson. Holding on to the pain was hurting *me*. When we hold on to past hurt, we think we are hurting those who hurt us. We believe our grudge is punishing them, when, in fact, we are hurting ourselves. The inability to forgive is choosing to drink poison yet expecting the other person to die. Backwards logic, right? Often times, you spend years holding grudges towards people who have not the slightest idea you are mad. While you are wallowing in pain, they have moved on. If you want to be the confident woman you have always wanted to be, commit to starting over with a clean slate. Once you are free from the shackles of the harsh words shared by others, you can rebuild your inner foundation with your own truth – with the opinion you hold true of yourself, created from a loving, whole, and truthful place.

I came to know Christ in my 20's. I found myself in an extremely depressed place. I was a young wife and mother in a new city and state while my husband worked long hours to provide for our family. One day, my mother-in-law came by the house and bluntly said, " You need to get out of this house. We are going to church on Sunday." I agreed. I went along with her suggestion because I didn't think much of it. "Church with my mother-in-law? Sure, I'll go," I thought. I attended church as a child, off and on, and frequented church with my best friend when I visited her, but I did not have a real relationship with Christ until the Sunday I attended with my mother-in-law.

I dressed my daughters in church-appropriate attire, got myself together, and off we went. During the sermon, I heard a dynamic message and suddenly felt something strange through-out my body, a feeling I never felt before. The only way I can de-scribe this new feeling was a hot, emotional sensation that radi-ated over my body. I looked around to see if anyone else was sweating or if it was just me. Well, it was just me. When the call was given for anyone who would like prayer to walk down the aisle, I really wanted to go but I didn't. We left church, and I was sure that my life would go back to normal... until my mother-in-law told me we are going back. When she spoke, I listened! So, back again we went. This time, it was a hot day in April. Every day is a hot day in Texas, really. Once again, the pastor preached an amazing sermon, but what I truly recall from that day is how I wrestled with myself about approaching the alter.

Would I go up this time?

Similar to the prior service, the invitation to approach the alter finally arrived. I dug my foot in the carpet, shuffling my feet, and that hot feeling came over my body once again. But this time, I could not sit still. I walked down the aisle for prayer, just to rid myself of this foreign feeling. The pastor (who has been my pastor ever since) looked me in the eyes and said, "The Lord told me to tell you that you will never be lonely again." I burst into tears. I had been so lonely, even in crowds of people. I had a wonderful husband, healthy, beautiful babies, and a supportive family, but something remained missing in my life. You cannot fill the voids in your life with people or things or expect to place people in a spot only Jesus can fill.

On that Sunday afternoon in April, I gave my life to Christ.

My new relationship with the Lord caused me to heavily reflect on my past – all the wrong choices I made and was currently making, too. As I studied His Word, I learned of His unending, perfect forgiveness of my sins. How can I possibly hold a grudge when He does not, and will never, hold a grudge against me? Colossians 3:12-13 reminds us, "So, as those who have been chosen of God, holy and beloved, put on a heart of compassion, kindness, humility, gentleness and patience; bearing with one another, and forgiving each other, whoever has a complaint against anyone; just as the Lord forgave you, so also should you." We make mistakes, daily, yet He gives us another chance at life. Several chances, actually. His forgiveness is everlasting. Christ is the ultimate example of forgiveness, and not only because He died for our sins. He also took the brunt of betrayal and hurtful comments from those closest to Him, yet He offered forgiveness: "But Jesus was saying, 'Father, forgive them; for they do not know what they are doing.' And they cast lots, diving His garments among themselves" (Luke 23:34). Jesus did not simply bark orders or shout commandments. His life shares perfect examples of God's Word applied to everyday living. So, we must follow suit, and by following suit, our hearts will be free from malice, no longer holding on to the weight of the past. Knowing our Savior graciously endured harsh words fills me with the strength to endure strife as well. Jesus never said forgiveness was easy, however, He did show the way to forgive, even in the midst of suffering. After all, my life is not about what others think of me but what He thinks of me. Living for an audience of One has set me free from the baggage of my past. I live to please Him, not please other people. At the end of the day, I am forgiven. So, I forgive. "Whenever you stand praying, forgive, if you have anything against anyone, so that your Father who is in heaven will also forgive you your transgressions" (Mark 11:25). After you make the decision to forgive others, the next step is to forgive yourself. Typically, the reason people have low self-esteem is due to the inability to forgive themselves. Low self-esteem often equates to built-up shame and pent-up anger, mainly the inability to let go. Shame regularly leads to feeling unworthy of love, and those negative feelings and thoughts are typically coupled with low self-esteem. You made mistakes, we all have, but you have not let yourself off the hook.

Why?

Why are you shackling yourself to your past, your mistakes, your flaws, or your pitfalls?

"I could have!"

"I should have!"

"Why didn't I?"

Those questions will put you in an early grave if you continue to explore them. By probing yourself with toxic questions that have absolutely no relevance to your life, questions that cannot change the past, you will continue to demean yourself until your self-esteem is less and less.

If you want to be the woman you always wanted to be, the

strong, powerful woman you have always envisioned, you must forgive the person you once were. We all make mistakes, but those mistakes do not define who you are. Your mistakes, or poor past choices, are lessons which should develop your strength and character, molding you into who you are destined to be. Give yourself permission to evolve without boundaries or a final due date. You are allowed to continually change, grow, and progress. In order to be all you can be, you have to remove the filter in which you see yourself. See yourself through Christ's eyes: "Therefore if anyone is in Christ, he is a new creation; the old things passed away; behold, new things have come" (2 Corinthians 5:17). He died for our sins, and His death paved the way for our identity to be free of shame and guilt.

Think of a child and his or her mother. The mother knows their child will make a mistake. Plenty of mistakes, actually. That's life – full of lessons, occasional back-pedaling, and evolution. A mother also understands that she is dealing with a child, a child who is learning and growing, a child who deserves grace on their quest to maturation. Well, the same level of compassion you would have for a child is the same level of compassion you need to have for yourself. Understand that what you once did may have been childish, but you are not perfect. You cannot be expected to live a perfect life. The goal of achieving perfection is a failing thought in itself! Instead, vow to make better choices in the future. Commit to choosing a different path rather than walking down the road which once led to disappointment and shame.

I have made many mistakes in my life, but in order to grow I had to understand how I got there. Use mistakes as teachers, not masters. A master tells you how to move, where to go, and how to act. Similarly, the inability to forgive has the same effect, causing a person to move and stop based on limiting beliefs and a lack of self-trust. Use your mistakes as valuable lessons. Review each mistake with fresh eyes. When you feel upset about a mistake you made, take a step back and dissect your decision.

How did I get there?

What was I feeling at the time?

How can I keep myself from repeating the same mistake?

Another choice keeping people stuck in the past or in the same position is not taking responsibility for mistakes, deciding to blame others instead. You cannot heal any situation you are unclear on. You can be blinded by the delusion that every bad thing that has happened to you has been someone else's fault. This position leaves you in the state of being a victim, pushing you away from healing, leaving you unclear about important matters. Placing the blame solely on someone else without looking in the mirror is a pathway to self-destruction. If you take the position of denial, refusing to acknowledge your shortcomings, you will not receive the freedom you need. Own your part, then let go. You will do better next time when presented in a similar situation.

Do you defeat yourself?

You are not a victim but a victor!

"But in all these things we overwhelmingly conquer

through Him who loved us" (Romans 8:37).

To be the confident woman you always wanted to be, you cannot see yourself as a victim. If you feel stuck in the area of taking personal responsibility, ponder these questions:

Did you allow yourself to be part of something you knew was wrong or potentially harmful and toxic?

Regarding love – if you are hurt by a failed relationship, did you overlook who that person showed you they were in the beginning?

Regarding friendship – if a friend betrayed you, did you participate in their negative conversations about other people? Remember, if they talk to you about others, they will talk about you to others, too.

Take inventory of yourself, completely and honestly, so you can pull yourself all the way out of the uncomfortable or shameful position you are in. Assess your faults and how your choices played a part in the way you are feeling. More times than not, we have a hand in our hurt. This conception is not stated for you to blame yourself but for you to get a clear understanding so these avoidable growing pains do not happen again or happen frequently.

For a long time, I blamed my daughter's father for leaving me with a baby to care for by myself. As I worked through my journey of forgiveness, I realized how I contributed to that situation. I made the choice to be with him. I picked him to have an intimate relationship with, and I had to take my portion of responsibility. I allowed myself to expect adult results from a childish situation. I had no one to blame for that but myself. I chose to forgive him, and I chose to forgive myself. "My heavenly Father will also do the same to you, if each of you does not forgive his brother from your heart" (Matthew 18:35).

Do not be held hostage anymore.

Refuse a self-hostage situation!

Your outlook regarding your mistakes, combined with how you have processed the opinions of others, puts a fuzzy, distorted filter on the person you see in the mirror. If you have chosen to harp on the poor choices you have made, continually punishing yourself for the past, reliving mistakes and pitfalls, allowing the negative opinions of others to permeate your mind, you will more than likely see an unrecognizable, unflattering reflection in the mirror. You will be staring at a person you deem unworthy and unfavorable – a person you do not recognize. Well, let's use the Windex of forgiveness and wipe that shame away. Clean the mirror and refocus on a new, shiny reflection – a reflection that projects self-love, confidence, and worthiness. People commonly say, "I will forgive but I will never forget," but when you do not forget, you are choosing to hold on to pain of the past, a pain that will remain in the back of your mind. Choosing not to forget is choosing not to forgive. Life is entirely too short. Refuse to look at a clouded reflection.

Let go!

Forgive.

Holding a grudge requires a great deal of energy. Choosing not to forgive requires deliberate thought and invested emotion. Grudges hold a lofty price tag – the price of peace. Wouldn't you rather use that energy on yourself to develop new practices of self-love and healthy thinking? I know I would.

Perhaps you want to forgive, but you are unsure how.

How can you actually forgive when hurt is involved?

How can you forgive when an apology was not offered?

How can you forgive when you are still furious or embar-rassed?

How can you forgive when you have not moved on?

My pastor once offered a great tip regarding how to forgive. He said, "If you want to forgive someone or something, stop talking about it."

Simple advice. Powerful, too.

Train your mind to stop talking about what brings you pain. That does not mean avoid your pain or avoid releasing. This advice means that you need to stop fixating on what has been done and said. Do not harp. Do not replay these situations or any of the "what if" questions. Allow yourself time to process what happened, or what was said, then release. Let go. Commit to di-gesting what happened without regurgitating. That is a seemingly gross analogy, but there is nothing pretty about continually choosing to revisit toxicity. Pray through your pain, speak to a therapist, or talk with a trusted loved one, but if you are replaying the past so you can remain in your feelings and feel justified in being wronged, you will stay stuck in those negative feelings forever. Remember, forgiveness is not for them. Forgiveness is for you. If you do not face the issues of your past, your issues will control your present.

Choosing to forgive and move on does not make you a pushover or a weakling. In fact, choosing to forgive qualifies you as stronger than the average! The more you understand the purpose of God's grace, the stronger you will be in your continual decision to forgive yourself and forgive others. By granting forgiveness, you are not excusing someone's behavior or turning a blind eye. What you are doing is putting a stop to a hostage situation. You are refusing to be held hostage by someone else. Moving forward with bricks on your back is extremely difficult. No matter how quickly you try to move forward, you will feel the weight on your shoulders.

Put the bricks down.

Leave them behind.

Forgive.

If Jesus is able to forgive those who violently nailed His body to the cross, I am confident we can forgive others who betray us, curse us, and hurt us. He suffered horrendous pain and torture, more than any of us could possibly bear to imagine, yet He held true to the values of God's intentions – granting forgiveness.

Try It on for Size

Make a list of the people who have hurt you, in any capacity – people who have caused you pain, a pain you have yet to forgive and forget or maybe just forget. Begin to journal about each situation. Journaling is a powerful tool of release which will move feelings from your heart to the page. As you journal, take some time to honestly reflect over these people and situations. Digest the details of your pain, and make the decision to forgive. Go through this process for each person on your list until you reach the end of your list.

Mirror Work

I forgive those who have hurt me, intentionally or unintentionally. I release those people, and the hurt, from my heart. I choose to freely move through the world so I can receive the blessings coming to me. I forgive myself for all the bad choices and mistakes I have made. I am free from all that un-forgiveness has to offer. I am free to move on and be my best self.

2 – SEE WHO GOD SEES

"Seeing yourself through the eyes of God gives you the clearest picture."

Who does God see when He sees you?

Do you believe He sees who other people see?

Do you believe He sees you as the mistakes you have made?

Do you believe He sees your flaws and shortcomings?

If you answered "yes" to any of those questions, allow me to assure you – you are completely wrong. In fact, you could not be further from the truth if you think any of those statements hold value. His love for you, and the way He sees you, is based on His unending mercy for you. "Blessed be the God and Father of our Lord Jesus Christ, who according to His great mercy has caused us to be born again to a living hope through the resurrection of Jesus Christ from the dead" (1 Peter 1:3a).

Your purpose on this Earth is not to convince anyone to love you. Spending your time and energy convincing others to love you is foolishly giving another person the power and control to determine your worth. Your worth was determined by God before you took your first breath of air: "Even before there is a word on my tongue, Behold, O Lord, You know it all" (Psalm 139:4). The unequivocal truth is that God sees you as fearfully and wonderfully made! You are covered in the blood of Jesus Christ, and, because of Him, He covers you in grace, love, and mercy, forever.

He made you!

He lives inside of you!

So how can something or someone He created not be beautiful or worthy? Many people are consumed by the need of approval, sacrificing their identity and purpose for the sake of attention: "Beware of practicing your righteousness before men to be noticed by them; otherwise you have no reward with your Father who is in heaven" (Matthew 6:1).

Remember when I told you that seeking attention comes with a hefty price tag? Jesus died for your sins so that you would know you are forgiven and worthy – you are worthy of grace, love, and forgiveness. Your identity is found in Christ, and your sins are washed away by His mercy. In His truth, you receive unconditional love and forgiveness. Only Jesus is the living Bread of life. Only in Him and through Him will we never go hungry. When you crave and seek Jesus, your need for man's approval will recede. If you refuse to believe that He sees you as His worthy child, remind yourself that He died on the cross for you, that your strongest desires can be fulfilled through Him. If dying on the cross does not constitute as the ultimate level of worthiness, I don't know what ever will. There is nothing you can do to make God love you any more or any less than He does in this moment. The love He bestows is unending, without limitations, and everlasting. If you are spending your time trying to gain the approval of others or please certain people, remind yourself that you have already gained the most valuable approval of all – God's approval. He sees the core of who you truly are and loves you despite your sins, habits, faults, and flaws.

Again, ask yourself – "Who does God see when He sees me?"

If your answer involves any element of negativity, stop yourself and start over. Rethink the answer to that question. Retrain your mind to know and believe you are His beloved:

> But when the kindness of God our Savior and
> His love for mankind appeared, He saved us,
> not on the basis of deeds which we have done
> in righteousness, but according to His
> mercy, by the washing of regeneration and
> renewing by the Holy Spirit" (Titus 3:4-5).

Knowing how God sees you will give you the tools to take your confidence to the next level. See yourself through the eyes of the One who made you. Just think – the creator of the universe, the heavens, and the Earth found that the world was missing something, and that something was you! You were purposefully and thoughtfully created. Your life is deliberate and valuable. There is only one of you, and He intended your life to be unique in its own right. Of all the people, animals, flowers, and creatures, God took the time to create and devise a specific plan... just for you!

You are precious.

You are a reflection of God.

He made you – He knows exactly who you are. God is not surprised by the way you speak. He is not surprised that you may start yelling when traffic moves slowly. He is not surprised by your triggers, your sins, or your shortcomings. He knows exactly what He made. Your job is to get comfortable with yourself. God is not mad at you for your past mistakes or decisions. He knew what you would do before you were born, yet He still made you! Not only did He make you, but He gave you purpose. Above all, He wants you to be happy with yourself. He did not intend for any of our lives to be lived in misery or despair. So, do not replace God's opinion of you for the opinions of others. At any point in time, their opinions should not outweigh His. He trumps all! The reason you cannot base your self-esteem on others is because the opinions of people are biased – they may feel threatened by you being all that God has called you to be. You may also find your popularity decreasing as you walk in your calling. Many people will discourage you out of fear you may surpass them. Nevertheless, God's calling trumps the opinions of others and the opinion you have of yourself.

Why?

Because He knows you better than you know yourself. He is the ultimate Creator. You must commit to changing your mode of thinking, and you must go easy on yourself in the process. If our ultimate Creator goes easy on you, why on Earth would you be hard on yourself? Humble yourself and accept God's unending grace and mercy. Give yourself grace when you fall short.

As I was working on this book, I found myself wondering a number of doubtful thoughts.

"Who are you, Monique?"

"Are you really trying to be an author?"

"Will anyone like this book?"

"Will this book be met with criticism and rejection?"

Negative thought after negative thought swirled around in my mind... until I took my own advice – I stopped my negative train of doubt and insecurity and reminded myself who I am: I am Monique Mays, I belong to God, and I am more than capable of delivering a manuscript that will change the hearts and minds of the masses.

Similarly, when you decide to be secure and intentional with your purpose, tests will arise. My tests came in many forms.

I was met with writer's block, feelings of doubt, and insecure thoughts. In retrospect, I know I came to a head with those challenges from the enemy because my purpose is so powerful. As I was cementing my foundation for this book, in a bold attempt to encourage you, I was faced with mental opposition. During this period of struggle, everything seemed to be going wrong. Me and one of my daughters started to struggle. We could not agree on anything, and she wanted to do the opposite of anything that mirrored me. A little rebellion, perhaps, and a bit of soul searching, too, it seemed. She expressed she was not happy and wanted me to let her be her. She began to act out, which is highly unlike her, and I could not understand where her change of heart came from. In my many roles, I am supposed to encourage women to love themselves, but the rejection I felt from my precious child took a hit at my self-esteem. Consequently, I continued to question myself. After many conversations with God, talks with a few trust friends, and several of tears, I got *it*! I was with my good friend in my prayer room, and boom, the realization hit me like a ton of bricks! I figured out my problem – I was equating who I was by my roles and respective titles. I am a wife, I am a mother, and I am a friend. There was the problem. I forgot that I am a child of God, first and foremost. When I had problems with my child, I quickly assumed I was a bad mother. When I had an issue in my marriage, I thought I was a horrible wife. If there was an issue with a loved one, I questioned myself as a friend. The enemy was making a valiant effort to infiltrate my closest relationships and stir insecurity in my life where he knows God had placed some of my greatest strengths. Through prayer is how I reached my break-through. I released the situation with my daughter and released my hurt feelings to God. My identity is found in Christ, not through my roles and titles. Christ is my Center and my Rock. My identity is found in Him. He never changes. He is a solid, safe place to stand. People change, but Jesus remains the same. My emotions change on a daily basis, but if I see myself as He sees me, I can remain steady and solid. He knows exactly who I am, not the persona I put out or the roles I am expected to fulfill. He knows me, not by the clothes I wear or the face that is seen in public, but the person I am in private – the total woman, the raw me. He knows the thoughts I think that I would not dare allow anyone to hear. He knows you and He knows me, and He loves you just the way you are, not fixed up or in the way you please or displease others, but at your core! Seeing yourself as God sees you means realizing you are not what others think of you or even the role you play in the lives of others, but what God thinks of you, and He believes you are awesome!

God had to remind me who I belong to through several different signs. He showed me who I am and that I can serve the world through this book. He used the situation with my daughter to show me a powerful revelation of who I am to Him. Through the strife with my daughter, He reiterated the importance of remaining focused on my strengths rather than assuming the problem always lies within me.

The enemy wanted me to feel insecure.

The enemy wanted me to use a question mark in the areas of my life that God placed a period.

The journey to being the confident woman you always wanted to be is a life-long journey. There may be moments when you think, "Wow, I'm finished. I am who I want to be." But God is always molding you and strengthening you. The enemy wants you to be complacent. He wants you to believe you are finished growing because the more you thrive, the harder it is for him to control you. So, you must remind yourself who you are and to whom you belong. Through prayer, the Lord guided my heart to Jeremiah 29:11: "'For I know the plans I have for you,' declares the Lord, 'plans for welfare and not for calamity to give you a future and a hope.'" I grasped on to this verse as a promise to myself, and these words quickly eased my doubts.

Your confidence soars from knowing and believing the ultimate power, the Creator, and He knows you are wonderful. The Bible says you are fearfully and wonderfully made, custom-made by the best of the best, the Most High. Embrace who He says you are. Jesus showed us we are to die for, literally!

We become quickly wrapped up in what we see on the outside, but you are so much more than what you see in the mirror. Find joy in the fact that God can see the end from the beginning. You can be whatever your heart desires, you just have to go to the One who created you to get your marching orders. You may look in the mirror and think to yourself, "I am not meant to be more than I am right now. I just can't do it," but God already knows the ending to your success story. He knows your capabilities and strengths... He just wants you to seek Him as you make your next move. Ask God to show you who He sees! Through studying His Word and spending time in prayer, you will discover who He sees, knows, and loves. You are intelligent, you are beautiful, and you are here for a purpose!

Try It on for Size

Commit to discovering what the Word of God says about you. Appoint a specific time and place to pray, and read the book of John, plus the additional passages listed below. The book of John shares exactly how much God loves us. Read the following passages and answer the following questions.

John 1:12

John 15:15

2 Corinthians 5:17

Ephesians 1:4

Ephesians 1:11

1 Thessalonians 1:4

Which of the above-listed scriptures struck you the deepest and why?

What does that particular verse mean to you?

How can you apply what you read to improving your self-esteem?

Is there a change you need to make in your life that reflects what you have read?

Mirror Work

I see myself clearly. God loves me, completely and without exception. I am a chosen vessel to bless this world. My life has a divine purpose. I know that my foundation is found in the One who created the foundation of the Earth. I am complete, I am loved, and I am a child of the King.

3 – MIRROR, MIRROR

"How you care for yourself is a direct reflection of your level of self-love."

"Beauty is only skin deep" – a common saying you may have heard a time or two (or ten). You may be thinking, "Here she goes with yet another cliché," but this statement holds true and always will. There is a reason why some clichés are timeless – they hold weight and meaning that resonate from generation to generation, the same way the Lord's Word resonates now and forever. Yes, beauty has a lot to do with outward appearance, but beauty is certainly applicable to a person's heart, far more than looks itself. But back to the physical – think of how you feel when you have on your best outfit and your hair and makeup are laid for the gods! You have a different type of walk and feeling compared to when you roll out of bed with your tangled hair all over your head.

We are not Beyoncé, we don't wake up like this!

A polished exterior requires effort. As you work on the beauty of your heart and mind, do not neglect the beauty of the outside. Self-care is important as well, very important, in fact... and not for reasons pertaining to vanity or the need to fit in or appease others. Instead, self-care is a reflection of self-love.

If you find your self-confidence declining, do a self-check on how you are choosing to take care of yourself:

- When is the last time I made myself a priority?
- Have I set aside time to be alone?
- When is the last time I felt beautiful and comfortable in my clothes?
- How have I been eating?
- Do I regularly feel beautiful?

Make self-care a priority, not only for the physical aspects, but for your health and mental well-being. When you look better, you feel better. Do not forget to schedule *you* into your schedule. Women often feel guilty for taking time for themselves. Let me assure you – there is absolutely nothing selfish about carving out personal time. In fact, if you do not take time for yourself, you will only remain in the mental state to give you and your loved ones an exhausted version of yourself. *That* is selfish, because you deserve to give yourself the best you've got! In order to give the best of who you are to others, and yourself, you must be the best version of yourself. Loving yourself is not selfish, it's self-full. Once you are full, you can flow into the lives of those around you. In life, you play several roles – you are a daughter, a friend, an employee, a companion, a student, and so much more. Think of those roles as cups on a table. For each cup, you have to pour a little of yourself into every one. Now imagine all the cups you have in your life. In my life, for example, I am a mother, a wife, a businesswoman, an author, a friend, a volunteer, and I wear a few other hats, too. Every person and every responsibility takes a little of who you are. That is why remaining full is vital. You cannot pour from an empty cup. In my own life, there are days I do not feel like getting dolled up. Sometimes, I don't even feel like getting out of my pajamas! On days like those, I definitely do not feel my best. I am just not prepared for the day. If I get a call from my children's school, I feel unprepared because I am not dressed. Scrambling to find a decent outfit to throw on affects my mood tremendously. When I am dressed, however, with my hair and makeup done, I feel more confident, prepared and ready to take on what the day has to offer. You want to feel confident, mentally and physically. You can only do that by giving the best to yourself. Think about the Proverbs 31 woman. She was amazing, she did everything! The scriptures say she dressed in fine linens and in purple. These were custom clothes, not disheveled garments. With all of her other tasks, she managed to make time to look good!

In my own life, I have been blessed to see a Proverbs 31 woman in the flesh. My grandmother, Juanita Wilson, was the epitome of hardworking yet poised and beautiful. For many decades, she ran multiple homes for the elderly. I would see her taking care of patients with the utmost care. She cooked, cleaned, and managed the business's finances. I was in awe of her work ethic. After her long hours of work, she would still look so beautiful. Her confidence made her shine. As a little girl, I would watch her get dressed up on Sunday mornings for church, with her hat and heels, and her elegance just oozed out of her pores. She was the most beautiful woman I have ever met. She knew the importance of not only being successful in business but also the importance of making time for herself.

Balance is key.

You can be a business owner, or a stay-at-home mother, and still make your appearance a priority.

If you don't believe that self-care is vital, deserved, and necessary, believe Jesus! Self-care is discussed, at length, in the Bible! Recharging to reach a place of emotional and spiritual stability is encouraged: "Come to me, all you who are weary and burdened, and I will give you rest" (Matthew 11:28).

Let's go over a few self-care tips that will help you feel just as good on the outside as you do on the inside.

First, drink water. Simple enough, right? Drinking more water is a fantastic first step toward being more confident because this step involves nourishment. Clearer skin and a flatter stomach will be your reward, especially when drinking lemon water because this combination detoxifies the body. Health experts recommend drinking half of your body weight in ounces. Purchase a cute, refillable water bottle and keep it with you so you can monitor your water intake. You definitely want to make healthy choices involving food and exercise, too. Do not neglect your sleep either. When you feel unhealthy or sluggish, feeling confident is difficult. Your mind will be tired, operating on a lack of sleep, inevitably making subpar decisions due to fatigue. Your body is a temple, housing the spirit of God. Treat your body well. Love it and make it pretty.

Now, let's take a walk through your wardrobe. When is the last time you went through your closet to see what fits and what has seen its last days? Set aside one day to sort through your clothes. Ask yourself what colors look best with your skin tone. Rediscover what pieces fit, because there is nothing worse than seeing a woman stuffed into something too small. Bend over, bend down, and lift your arms – is everything covered? Do any pieces stretch over areas because they are too tight? If so, place the item to the side and donate it. When shopping, do not assume certain pieces will not look good. Instead, try them on! Something may look one way on the hanger but completely different on your body. Trying on your clothes will also save you from having to take the item back because the number size did not match the fit. So, give it a go! Try on that dress you may assume will not look great. I bet you will be pleasantly surprised. More importantly, do you have the basics? The basics are staple items essential to any wardrobe. Owning these pieces will actually save you a great deal of money in the long run because you can mix and match other items with these staples instead of buying new clothes each season. Here is a list of quality essentials:

- White button-up shirt
- Flattering pair of dark wash jeans
- Little black dress (*no explanation needed*)
- A pencil skirt
- A fabulous pair of heels
- A classic pair of flats
- Classic blazer

Once you sort through your closet, make a list of clothing items you need. Remember, these are necessities, not wants. So, those trendy, six-inch stilettos you've had your eye on may have to wait because this list involves staples that will remain in your closet for years to come. Creating this list will help you the next time you go shopping. You will have a better focus on what you need rather than aimlessly buying pieces you probably won't wear.

Oh, and do not forget to accessorize! You can take a plain outfit to the next level with some beautiful accessories. Rule of thumb: One statement piece per outfit. If you are wearing large earrings, choose a simple bracelet and skip the necklace. If you are wearing a large statement necklace, opt for stud earrings. You never want to look like you are wearing everything from your closet. Before leaving your home, I want to make sure you have a full look put together, and integrating essential wardrobe pieces with a fabulous accessory is a no-fail plan.

As a young girl, I was always the tallest girl in my class. My height made me extremely insecure, so I would walk hunched over in hopes that my height would not be so obvious. Kid logic, right? Until one day, in sixth grade, my stepfather took me shopping. We went to a few different clothing stores and ended our trip at a local shoe store. There they were – a pair of heeled, blue, jelly sandals. If you grew up in the late nineties, you know exactly what I'm talking about. I asked, "Can I try them on?" He quickly obliged. I excitedly grabbed the jellies off the shelf and tried them on. I wobbled over to the mirror. I was about eleven years old, so heels were not my forte. I looked at myself in the mirror, with my normal hunch in posture, but the added height of the shoes caused me to stand up straight. I looked in the mirror again, and the height I was so ashamed of was suddenly replaced with a feeling of pride. I saw myself with more height than I naturally had, and I loved it. I pranced around the store, trying to get my ankles accustomed to this new feeling. I asked my stepfather if he would purchase them. With the look of sheer excitement on my face, he could not resist. I got home and began practicing my walk, confidently posing in the mirror. My blue jellies became my favorite accessory. I finally saw my height as beautiful. So, don't tell me what a good pair of heels can't do! To this day, you will rarely catch me without a pair of heels on. They are essential to my wardrobe and a reminder to love my height, even if I tower over everyone else, which is fine by me.

While we are on the subject of essentials, let's talk about undergarments. Sure, these pieces are not seen by the public, but well-fit undergarments are imperative if you want to leave the house feeling comfortable and confident. Your bras should fit well and appropriate per the top you choose to wear. If your current bras are ill-fitting, you can go to any bra or lingerie store and let them measure you. Many times, we are unknowingly not wearing our proper size. Your straps should not dig into your shoulders, and your skin should not spill over the sides of the bra. These are telltale signs you are in the wrong size. If you choose to wear a spaghetti-strap top, wear a strapless bra underneath. Appropriate undergarments are essential. You want to make sure you do not ruin an outfit, or, more importantly, you do not want to ruin your confidence with ill-fitting undergarments, including shapewear. If you want to wear something formfitting, but feel a bit uncomfortable by the snugness of the garment, use a girdle or a shaper. These are a girl's best friend, I promise. These pieces flatten the tummy and smooth out unwanted indentations. Make sure your shapewear fits well also. It should be snug enough to pull you in but not so tight that your body spills out. You want to be snatched but able to breathe.

Looking well-put together has its perks, but nothing can take the place of good hygiene. I have heard women say, "I'm so busy with these kids, I haven't showered in days!" This is a prime example of not making yourself a priority. Listen, I am a mom. I understand. Time is limited. As much as we would like to kick back and take a nice, hot bubble bath, time does not always permit. However, your hygiene is a major sign of self-love. You are a woman, your scent is integral to who you are. So, take the time to shower and smell your best. Find a body wash that is not overpowering yet gets the job done. You do not want to smell like you just ran through the forest or rolled around in a watermelon patch. Less is more. Keep those scented soaps off of your lady parts, too.

Do you want to take self-care to the next level?

Exfoliate, exfoliate, exfoliate!

Exfoliation is the process of removing dead skin cells from the top layer of your skin. I have to admit, I am an exfoliating junkie. I love nothing more than super soft skin. There are two options for exfoliation. You can buy body scrubs or you can make them yourself. If you opt to make them, all you need is olive oil and brown sugar (or sea salt). Scoop the scrub with your fingers and rub a quarter-sized portion over your body in circular motions. This will give your skin a nice, healthy glow. Exfoliation is an extra step in hygiene, but you are worth the time! After all, what woman does not want to be baby soft? Exfoliate at least twice a week. Let folks see that God-given glow that was buried under those dead skin cells. I want you to shine, honey! So, do not forget about your skin.

You will also want to find a skincare routine that works for you. Your steps should include cleansing, toning, treating, and moisturizing. In terms of skin, we are all at different stages. Your skin is unique, and there is not a one-size-fits-all skin care plan. Some of us need acne treatments whereas some want anti-aging solutions. This will be a trial-and-error process, so do not be discouraged.

There are four skin types: normal, combination, dry, and oily. Find a product line specific to your type. You can determine your skin type through free resources such as YouTube or Google. If a quality skincare regimen is in your budget, make time to see a dermatologist or an esthetician. The most important objective is finding a regimen that works best for you.

From your head to your toes, self-care is vital, and your hair is your crown. Whether your hair is long or short, braided or shaved, love on your hair. Find a style you can maintain and a style that suits you well. Follow a wash-and-condition routine to maintain your hair's moisture and a healthy scalp. At night, you want to keep your hair moisturized. Add a satin scarf or satin pillow case to your collection, if need be. The satin material will keep your hair from drying out. Similar to your skincare routine, you will need to try different products to find what works best for you. Do not be afraid to try new products. You never know what you may like or what will agree with your hair. If you choose to wear extensions, be gentle to your natural hair underneath. You do not want to take your extensions out and find nothing there. Treat your hair with the utmost care, and it will serve you well.

Self-care shows the world that you value yourself. Consequently, others will treat you accordingly, too. One more point of advice, since we are speaking of head-to-toe care – buy a pumice stone. Do not be that woman with cracked heels. If you are able, make bi-weekly pedicure appointments. If you cannot, make sure to take the time to paint your nails and keep them soft. A quick tip – place Vaseline on your feet and cover with socks. You will wake up with smooth feet. This is economical and reaps amazing results.

Let's talk makeup, shall we? Makeup is meant to enhance the natural beauty you already have. Makeup is not intended to transform your look unless you are an actress playing a role or it's Halloween. Don't get me wrong, I love a good beat, but you do not want to go overboard. If you find yourself needing to completely transform yourself, you either need to go back to the section on skincare or begin to love the skin you're in. I recommend the latter.

First, find a quality, smooth foundation. Make sure your foundation matches your skin tone. Go to any makeup counter and they will gladly match your complexion. Remember, blending is your friend. During application, make sure you blend your foundation down your neck so your makeup does not give the allusion of a mask covering your face. You will also need a good setting powder, mascara, and primer. Makeup is actually a lot of fun, so look around and find lip colors you like, as well as highlighters, blushes, and eyeshadows. Makeup is an adventure. Have fun and express yourself!

Most importantly, when discussing the body, please make sure you book annual checkups. Your health is key to vitality! A healthy body is of the utmost importance, not only for yourself, but for the people in your life. You are loved and valued! Your loved ones want you around as long as possible. So, you need to stay on top of your health. Many of the diseases women suffer from, such as breast cancer, ovarian cancer, and cervical cancer, can be prevented or effectively treated with early detection.

Make time for your beauty and make time for your body. These acts of self-care will boost your confidence in a profound way!

Self-care tips:
- Drink plenty of water
- Make healthy food choices
- Exercise regularly
- Have a skin and body care routine
- Exfoliate
- Find a hairstyle you love and maintain it.
- Wear clothes that make you smile and compliment your shape
- Find a makeup routine, if any, to fit your schedule, and enhance your natural beauty
- Take care of your nails and toes
- Schedule annual check-ups.

Try It on for Size

Thoroughly purge your closet of anything too small, worn out, or unrepresentative of who you are. Create a self-care routine for yourself, too. If you typically neglect yourself, set specific dates and times in your calendar. You want to hold yourself accountable. Also, schedule your annual checkups.

Mirror Work

I am choosing to take the best care of my body, the best care I ever have. I commit time and effort to my appearance and my physical well-being. I value my body. I am housing the spirit of God within me. When I step out into the world, I am well-dressed and confident. I am secure and proud of the body I have.

4 – NEW WORDS, NEW LIFE

"Words are seeds. Be mindful of what you are planting."

Speak new life into existence by retraining your words. What you say about yourself is significantly more powerful than what anyone else says about you. So, what are you saying to yourself about yourself?

Are you beating yourself up with self-inflicting words after a hard day at work?

Are you scolding yourself for something that happened in the past?

Are you kicking yourself while you are already down?

Are you discrediting yourself instead of encouraging yourself?

Remember, if you tell yourself what you are not, or what you will never be, you will be just that.

The Bible tells us that life and death are in the power of the tongue. Be careful how you think; your life is shaped by your thoughts (Proverbs 4:23). You must control your internal dialogue in order to change your life for the better. We speak thousands of words, daily, and fail to realize that words are seeds. When you speak, those seeds are planted into the garden of your life. Consequently, those seeds sprout and flourish, only if your words are positive and uplifting. "Death and life are in the power of the tongue, And those who love it will eat its fruit" (Proverbs 18:21).

When you degrade yourself, badger yourself, or compare yourself, you are planting seeds of self-doubt, anxiety, and low self-esteem. What you should be doing is planting seeds of love, confidence, and strength. You deserve to have a garden of positivity in your life, not weeds and dead plants. If you stand in front of the mirror and think negative thoughts, or complain about various circumstances in your life, you are planting seeds of toxicity that will blossom into poison.

The mind has an interesting way of working. While you are speaking negative words on a consistent, repetitive basis, your mind is taking notes. Your subconscious believes anything you tell it, so if you repeat negative thoughts, your mind will find a way to make those negative thoughts come true. Basically, the subconscious mind will turn those thoughts into reality. Instead of speaking negatively about yourself, practice feeding yourself positive words and words of affirmation. Replace what you would normally say with a compliment. The Bible encourages the standard of replacement:

> Finally, brethren, whatever is true, whatever is honorable, whatever is right, whatever is pure, whatever is lovely, whatever is of good repute, if there is any excellence and if anything is worthy of praise, dwell on these things" (Philippians 4:8)

Fixating on weaknesses, past mistakes, or insecurities is not what God wants you to focus on. Instead, accept you are a glorious child of God, and hone in on how God is able to move in your life, even in times of doubt and weakness. Raise your confidence by allowing God to restore your mind. After all, "Your life is shaped by your thoughts" (Proverbs 4:23). Repeat the following affirmations, daily, to instill a newfound confidence into your inner most being:

I am worthy.
I am capable.
I am intelligent.
I am special.
I am precious.
I am gifted.
I am loved.

Those affirmations, consciously optimistic words of positivity, will manifest in to positive life changes, and you will begin creating better situations and circumstances.

Has anyone ever told you that something you said helped them without you knowing? You can speak life into someone without knowing your impact, which is why speaking from an encouraging, loving place is vital. I vividly remember an experience from high school, when someone spoke life into me without knowing the impact they had in my life. About one week before the homecoming dance, during my junior year of high school, my pregnant belly was definitely noticeable.

"I really wish I could go to the homecoming dance," I longingly told my Grannpy.

I knew there were not going to be many more dances in my future, especially after I give birth.

"Well, why aren't you going, sweetheart?" he asked.

I told him I did not have a dress to wear to the dance.

So he asked, "Do you have an old dress you could wear that may fit?"

I only had the black homecoming dress I wore my sophomore year. With my new baby bump, I could not fit in that dress anymore.

"Just bring me the dress," he kindly prompted.

My Granppy happened to be a tailor, so letting the dress out a bit was only a five-minute job for him, and he did just that! I remember how insecure I felt while getting measured. As the tape measure covered my growing stomach, self-doubting thoughts flooded my mind. I was not feeling confident, but I toughed out the fitting and ended up with a well-fitted dress. I had my dress and got some blonde hair bonded in. Then, I placed some rhinestones across my bangs. Hey, wait, don't judge! It was the early 2000's! We had some crazy trends back then that we swore were cool. So, there I went, off to the homecoming dance. I was feeling fabulous in my dress, and I was ready to have a good time.

When a woman is pregnant, she frequently uses the bathroom, and I was no exception. I went to the bathroom several times during the homecoming dance. One particular time, on my way to the bathroom, I happened to pass by a group of teachers and other adults. I could not help but notice their judgmental stares, and I heard a few comments, too.

"What is she doing here?"

"Oh, that's such a shame."

Hearing those comments crushed my soul. I mean, I was already battling with my confidence, so to hear my teachers and other adults add fuel to my self-doubting fire was too much to bear. I obviously knew I was pregnant. The entire student body did, too. They pointed out the obvious, but in a cruel manner.

One of the teachers at school, Ms. Andino, noticed my sullen face as I was coming out of the bathroom, and she stopped me. Ms. Andino was not one of my teachers, but she was the "fun" teacher in school. You know, the teacher all the kids try to hang out with in her classroom.

"Hold your head up, Monique," she encouragingly said. "You will prove them all wrong!"

I wiped my tears and went on to stay for the remainder of the dance. Ms. Andino never knew that what she said that night showed me the power of encouraging words. I went on to do exactly as she said. Not only that, but I proved them all wrong, months later, when I walked across the stage to accept my honors diploma. Ms. Andino spoke life into me that fateful night, and you have the ability to do the same. You hold the power to not only help others but help yourself through positive self-talk. Hold your head up and prove them wrong! Speak life into yourself and the life of others. Wherever you are, thank you, Ms. Andino! You showed me the meaning and importance of speaking life into another human being – a vital act of self-love and demonstration of respect to others.

Who you are is based on the accumulation of words you have spoken over your life.

"Higher education is within your reach! You can do it!"

"Ask your boss for a raise. You deserve it!"

"Pursue your hobby as a potentially lucrative side business. Your effort and time will be worth it!"

If you want a new life, use new words!

Shed the negative, doubtful words you have employed in the past. Those words have not and will not work for the betterment of your life. Truth be told, words have the power to do one of two things: build you or break you. So, be very mindful of what words you are taking in. What seeds are you feeding your mind and body? Because you will eat the fruit of those seeds, whether positive or negative. On a deeper level, until you shed the negative, doubtful words you are accustomed to using, you will continue cursing the blessings God has in store for you. Remember, He has plans to prosper you, so refuse to go against His great plans.

Furthermore, do not make general statements. Avoid declarations such as "I will never be happy" or "I will always be broke" because those words will become your reality. Feeding yourself negative words will result in a body full of harmful, damaging thoughts, and worse, actions. Choosing the right words are vital in building strong self-esteem. Remember, with each word you speak, you are planting seeds into your life. If the words are not the type of harvest you want in your life, change your thought process to reap a new, fruitful harvest. Retraining your mind to speak positivity takes continual effort and constant awareness. Retraining your mind takes time, time to break the pattern of what you are used to. If you have always spoken negatively, your habit will not change overnight. The transition from positive to negative requires awareness – you have to learn to hear yourself. Many times, we rattle off words and do not pay attention to what we are actually saying. Take time, each day, and think about the words you have spoken – what you have said to yourself, to others, and about others. You cannot change something you are not aware of. This journey requires introspection and honesty. During this process, do not be too hard on yourself. We all do it – say words we do not mean – and many of us have been doing this unhealthy practice for so long that we do not even realize when we are speaking in a damaging way. This is why becoming self-aware is vital – to help you become the woman you want to be, the woman you deserve to be.

If you discover you are not having the experiences in life that you want, do a thorough word evaluation.

What have you been saying?

What type of results have you been reaping?

Are you feeding your mind with positive materials and thoughts?

Perhaps you did not land the job you had your eye on because you never deemed yourself worthy of applying. Maybe you did not accept the lunch invitation to join a new group of women because you were too nervous to befriend new ladies. Or, did you forgo your dream of trade school because you were too nervous of what other people would think about choosing trade school over a four-year college? Well, you have the power to dig up the words you have planted, place down new seeds, and reap more fruitful plants of life. The garden of your life is nothing to play with!

A few years ago, my husband and I decided we wanted to buy a house. Through our home-buying journey, I learned how important my words were. One day, I decided to make a shift in words, no longer saying, "We want to buy a house," but instead, "We are currently buying a house." We did not have a loan, a relator, or a down payment at the time, but I kept saying, "We are buying a house." I did research regarding different neighborhoods and floor plans, and I looked at the homes I wanted to buy with no idea of how it would happen. The words you speak are not the only words of importance. Written words are valuable, too. I wrote in a little notebook, claiming we would own a home before the last day of that year. I continued to say those words and write them, too. After about one month, our situation began to shift. We found a lender, we began saving for a down payment, and we found a builder for the home I had been eyeing for months. We put action behind our chosen words, and that is how our miracle occurred. Gardens and harvests do not grow without effort. Reaping requires effort, thought, planning, and consistency. As I have said before, your words have power, but how much power depends on your spirit. Do you have faith that what you are saying is going to come true? Your faith muscles have to be strengthened. The stronger your spirit, the stronger and quicker your words will manifest. Through a clear, solid spirit, words flow quickly and fluidly. As you are working on purposefully choosing your words, simultaneously work on your spirit. A solid spirit knows what it is saying and believes what it says! The belief in your words, and their ability to change your life, is the key to believing in what you say. "Truly I say to you, whoever says to this mountain, 'Be taken up and cast into the sea,' and does not doubt in his heart, but believes that what he says is going to happen, it will be granted him" (Mark 11:23).

Ten days before the end of that year, we closed on our dream home!

You want to make sure that the power you create by using your words is used for the edification of others. Be mindful in using your words for good and not evil, to lift up and not tear down. Talking negatively about people, and gossiping about other women, says more about your character than about the person you are gossiping about, no matter how badly you may deem their character or actions. You should be so busy getting your life together that you do not have the time to speak poorly of someone else. Every bad word you speak about others actually brings negativity to yourself. Worse, by speaking poorly of someone else, you are revealing your insecurities. Confident, loving people do not discuss people; they discuss ideas, dreams, and plans. You also block your blessings when speaking hurtful words about others. Instead, use your words to congratulate other people for their accomplishments. Those words open you up to receive the same blessings.

If you can learn to be genuinely happy for others, and speak goodness into their lives, the more goodness you will receive. One sign of a woman with solid self-confidence is that she is able to compliment other women without feeling lesser than. If you see someone with an outfit or hairstyle you like, tell them! Those sorts of compliments make you so much more attractive, inside and out, because sharing those uplifting words prove you are secure within. When you are secure in yourself, you can pour in to someone else's self-confidence without thinking it takes away from your own.

Try It on for Size

Carry out this exercise for one week.

Begin your day with prayer. Ask God to show you what type of words you have been using. Have they been for your benefit or your detriment? I want you to become intentional with your words. Make believe that every word you speak will automatically come true. Make believe you are the woman you speak of. I want you to look in the mirror and speak to the woman you want to be, as if you are her in that very moment. Remind yourself what you have accomplished, and tell yourself all of the wondrous goals you are capable of achieving. When you continually do this, you will appear significantly different when you look in the mirror. In reality, you are her. You just don't know it yet.

Mirror Work

When I speak, I am conscious of the words I release. I will use my words to uplift myself and others. I believe in the power of my words. I only use words to express love, bring joy, and speak positive change. I am the master of my words, and I use specific, purposeful words to create the life I want to have.

5 – FRIENDSHIP EVALUATION

"Friendship is not a spectator sport."

Who surrounds you?

Do you know the difference between a friend and an acquaintance?

Are the people in your inner circle trustworthy, loving, supportive, and honest?

What qualities are imperative to have as a friend?

What qualities do you look for in a friend?

Do your current relationships promote positive and healthy interactions?

The people we surround ourselves with have a lot to do with how we feel about ourselves. Healthy relationships are a form of self-love, equating to positive self-esteem. Unhealthy relationships reflect unhealthy habits, typically having to do with a lack of self-love. If you made a list of the people you deem friends, would you consider those people encouragers or discouragers? If you are constantly feeling down about yourself, examine your company. Relationships are a sure sign of how you feel about yourself, how you view yourself, and what you think you deserve.

The people you choose to have in your life will either push you towards the woman you want to be or drag you away from her. If they are doing the latter, that is because those people do not want to see you doing better, especially better than them, or they are unaware that their insecurities are rubbing off on you. Either way, your job is to protect your peace. The Bible clearly says to avoid evil companions and that bad company corrupts good. Remember, you have the choice of who you will give a front row seat to your life.

People in your life can be placed in three categories:

1. Nosebleed Seats
2. General Admission
3. VIP.

Allow me to break these sections down to help you put these concepts into perspective, and, consequently, provide you with the knowledge to group your friends accordingly.

1. Nosebleed Seats

If you think about a concert or sporting event, there are different tiers of seats. Naturally, when purchasing a ticket for a concert or show, we want to sit as close as possible so we can enjoy the view. That is not the case with this section. The people in nosebleed seats want to see the show or the game, but they do not want to pay a great deal to attend. So, they purchase the cheapest available tickets. They do not really love the artist or have a loyalty to the team. Many just want to say they were there, or they want to be present for a good time. In relation to your life, the people sitting in the nosebleed seats do not love you or have a strong loyalty to you, either. They are not committed to sitting close to the main stage (you) because proximity makes no difference to these people. They simply want to be around in case something happens, whether that something is entertaining or dramatic or even disastrous. They want entertainment. They want the experience, regardless of depth or capacity. They want to be around but not in a beneficial or purposeful way. Their intent veers on the side of nosy rather than concerned. They do not mind speaking badly of you, or being around people who speak badly of you, because they are so far from center stage that they do not think you can hear them.

One benefit of being in the nosebleed section is that the spectators have an easy exit. They are close to the door. They do not have to battle crowds. If something happens to go wrong, they can exit before anyone else. Do not expect these people to stick around when life gets tough. Expect them to be the first to exit.

MONIQUE MAYS

The problem with the nosebleed section is they can't see the show as clearly as the other attendees because they are seated far from the stage. So, they make assumptions about what is going on. They may see you, but that does not give them the space or privilege to know you, especially on a deeper level.

Evaluate your friends.

Do you have someone in your life who is not interested in sacrificing anything for you? They will not give any of their time or resources. They feel that offering time, energy, or support is just too much. They may expect you to swim an ocean for them but refuse to jump a tiny puddle for you.

Are they too busy when you need them, so they make a quick exit?

Do they want to witness your drama, pitfalls, or struggles but choose to remain at a distance so they do not have to support you through the hard times?

If you found yourself nodding your head to any of these descriptions, you just may have a nosebleed-section "friend." Let them stay there, watching your life from afar. In fact, be thankful those people are at a healthy distance because having those folks up close would be anything but healthy.

2.   General Admission

The people in the General Admission section are typically seated anywhere from the middle area of the arena or stadium to the

88

front row of the venue, similarly to where these people are positioned in your life, too. Categorically, these people range between what you may consider an acquaintance to who you may consider a friend. The people sitting in this section may be folks you talk to often. They know you well, and they are present in your life. In fact, they know your birthday and attend all of your events.

You may have known these people for many years, and they may have been supportive during some important times in your life. However, do not be fooled by time, especially when referring to friendships. Just because you stand outside for weeks at the ticket booth does not mean you will get a ticket. You just might miss the show.

I remember, all too well, a childhood friendship I had for many years, well into adulthood, however, we had grown apart. We knew little, if anything, about each other as we progressed through adulthood. I held on to the friendship, solely because we had known each other for so long, which is a rather common, yet unhealthy, practice. Many of us hold on to what used to be. Our friendship had expired, but we made excuses for why we were not as close as we once were.

Have you ever held on to a relationship you knew was over?

Did that person show you they were not willing to put any effort in but you kept them around anyway?

That is what happened in this particular friendship, or lack thereof. After many years of unhealthy patterns and interactions,

I decided our relationship had to come to an end. In the most uncomfortable conversation I ever had, I told her, "I'm sorry, but we really aren't friends, we have just known each other for a long time."She was not at all happy with my blunt approach, but I knew it needed to be done. Time without effort is not worth the time. Similarly, there are people in your life who have been around for a while but may not stay for the long haul. These people do not receive admission for simply hanging around. General Admission is tricky because these people will actually pay for a seat. They will answer the phone when you call, and they like to be in your company. Some may even pay more to be closer to you, too. Consequently, you may confuse your General Admission friends with your VIP's, but trust and believe they are not the same.

The difference?

General Admission friends have a limit. Yes, they want to be present, but only if the cost is not too high. They will go along with your ideas, as long as your idea does not cost them anything extra (time, energy, or money). These are the people that will leave if they do not like the show any longer. After all, they did not shell out a large sum of money to attend. They do not want you to change because they have become comfortable with who you are. They are not necessarily harmful or toxic people, but, at the same time, you must know they are General Admission – people meant to be acquaintances, or serve a purpose, reason, or season in your life. General Admission is not VIP!

Another way to distinguish this category from the others is realizing how happy you feel to tell these people the good news in your life. Gauge your feelings. Truthfully face your emotions.

Are you excited to tell them about the fantastic changes happening in your life or do you hesitate because you do not know if they will genuinely feel proud?

Are these people some of the first you call when you earn a raise or promotion?

Do you find yourself telling these people when you have relationship troubles or do you shy away because you are not exactly sure if they can be trusted?

Are you wildly excited to let them know you got approved for the house you've had your eye on?

Do they even know about that house in the first place?

If you find yourself hesitating when answering these questions, even for a second, you know that these particular people are not in the VIP section of your life. If you feel the need to stop feeling happy for a few seconds, or ceasing to celebrate a proud moment in your life, you must understand that this is for a reason. Your gut is not steering you wrong. These feelings are a direct reflection of the position these people have in your life and must remain in. Based on their reaction, you can get a clearer picture of their place. General Admission ticket holders are not granted access to VIP just because. So, they should not be issued the perks, insight, and privilege to having close access to your life either.

3. VIP

The people in the VIP section are a person's most loyal supporters. They are the ride-or-die fans! This group will be your smallest group, but that is perfectly okay. Rain or shine, these people are not only in attendance, but they are front and center, rooting you on. Whether you are popular and loved or hardly acknowledged, they will buy a front row ticket. My grandfather always told me that if I have one or two good friends, I would be extremely blessed.

Your VIP's have backstage access to your life, as they should, because they have proved their loyalty, dedication, and love. They are the people who happily see you outside of the concert or sporting event when you are feeling down, under the weather, or when your face is not all made up yet. They love you at your worst. They will defend you, in and out of your presence. Your VIP's want to see you win. VIP attendees get the benefits of being close to you because they have proven their loyalty and love. My best friend has a saying that I love. She says, "What you whisper in my ear doesn't get said aloud." She is definitely my most trusted ear! It is not just how a person treats you when they are in your presence but also when you are not around. Can you trust that the secrets or dreams you share will stay with them and not become public news? Trust is the biggest requirement to a VIP relationship. Effort is also vital to this type of connection. What are they willing to give to show you they want to be in your life just as much as you want to be in theirs? Just like the VIP tickets they purchase, they will give all they have to be part of your life. These people are your safe places to retreat to when you make a mistake. They will tell you the truth, but in the same breath, they will share constructive, honest criticism. *VIP's are not yes-men.* They will not sit back and watch you make a fool of yourself. I am blessed to have a VIP section in my life that will check me when I get out of line. Many times, I speak before I think so they reign me in before I get myself in trouble. VIP friends will also make sure you are on your top of your look. Check the pictures they post on social media. Do they look great and you look crazy? They will not allow that. They will tell you, "Girl, that shirt is too small" or "Your feet are hanging over your sandals!"

You need these people. These people will be there forever. Treat your VIP section well. After all, to have a friend, you must be a friend, and these people certainly deserve the friendship they are selflessly giving you.

Check what seat you are in among other people's lives. You cannot expect to be treated like a VIP when you treat others like nosebleed-seaters. Sometimes, we fixate on how we are treated that we forget how we treat other people. That is a selfish mentality, if you live your life expecting to be treated amazingly yet you are not reciprocating. Consequently, your friendships will remain at the nosebleed level. I expect to be treated in the manner I treat you. This concept has ended many friendships in my life. On the other hand this concept has also caused me to have a some genuine lifelong friends as well!

One reason your friendships are so important is because those relationships will keep you at the level they are at and striving toward reaching. "Do not be deceived: 'Bad company ruins good morals'" (1 Corinthians 15:33).

Your company can cause you to do things that you may not normally choose to do, causing you to go against your standards or values because that is who you choose to hang around and those are the choices they make. You have to love yourself enough to know who should and should not be in your company. You must decide who deserves to have the type of friendship you have to offer. You also need to be in the company of those who are positive and doing great things in their own life. Many times, your friends can be an inspiration and motivation for you to make positive changes in your own life. You never want to be the smartest one in the crew. You all should be able to learn from each other. Reciprocity is vital. No nosebleeds allowed!

Speaking of nosebleed attendees, do not allow the opinions of these folks to tear down your self-esteem. The truth is, they will not be in attendance long enough to see the end of your show! Not only that, but they see what they want to see. Meaning, they are committed to seeing you through their perception only and not through a truthful, complete lens. So, be wise about what you share and to whom. Do not put yourself in the position to feel hurt or betrayed by telling General Admission friends all about your dreams. They will not understand. Or, if they do understand your dreams, they may not whole-heartedly support. Instead, wisely invest your energy and time. Cherish and love your VIP friends. You will need them as you push towards the goal of being the woman you always wanted to be.

Try It on for Size

Make a list of the people in your life, and assign each person a seat. Do not assign their respective seat based on how long you have known them but by what they have shown you, experienced with you, taught you, and so forth. Take another sheet of paper and divide the page in two sections. On the right side of the paper, list the positives each person brings to your life. On the left side, identify the negatives. Be honest, and base your answers on the reality of each friendship. Go through everyone on your list and ask yourself, "Does this person positively impact my life or is this person a negative distraction? These lists will certainly put your relationships in perspective, only if you are honest and forthcoming.

Mirror Work

I choose to have uplifting, loving, and caring people in my life. I base my friendships off of the truth and experience. I choose to give my time and energy to those who make my life better, pushing me to improve and grow, loving me for who I am. I am a quality friend. I treat my friends well, I am trustworthy, and I cherish those I consider friends.

6 – SETTING STANDARDS

"If you do not draw a line, it will be crossed every time."

Standards are the measure by which you establish your norm. We all have standards – what we will and will not tolerate.

What is the importance of setting standards?

Why do we need to establish standards?

Please note – people will treat you the way you allow them to. If there is no line to cross, your boundaries will inevitably be pushed. Your self-esteem guides and establishes the standards you set for yourself and other people. If you love yourself, wholly and truly, your standards will reflect respective boundaries. On the other hand, if your self-esteem is fragile or wavering, your boundaries will more than likely be nonexistent or poorly established.

During my teenage years, I had a major problem with setting standards. Setting standards was a challenge. In fact, I did not have a set line that was too far for other people to cross, and because of my lack of boundaries, I made several choices I am not proud of. I let friends walk all over me. I allowed boys to have a good time with me without thinking of the consequences. I smoked, drank alcohol, and was basically out of control. At the same time, I was attempting to maintain a good-girl image to those closest to me. I feared their disapproval over my own disapproval. I had let myself go, and I was a willing participant! I would put on my best face in front of those I felt would be disappointed, but privately, I honestly did not care. I would do whatever and say whatever. To me, it was okay. Your standards are not only what you allow other people to do to you but what you allow yourself to do.

If you want to be a healthy woman, you will maintain a standard of healthy eating and you will make time to exercise.

If you are a Christian woman, the standard by which you live will be according to your faith and God's Word.

If you want to be respected and well-regarded in the work place, you will treat your coworkers with respect, value deadlines, and give your all to each task.

Setting standards for other people keeps your life in order because people understand how far they should and should not go. They will have a clear understanding of how to treat you, what you will forgive, and what is completely disallowed.

Lying?

Unacceptable.

Gossiping about you?

Intolerable.

Demeaning you?

Forbidden.

Tearing down your dreams?

Absolutely not.

More important than establishing standards is following through with them. You must keep the standards you choose to establish. Do not compromise your standards to be in the company of other people. Those people are not company you want to keep in the first place. Do not compromise your standards to make someone else comfortable. The truth is, you will never be comfortable with those folks no matter how at ease you make them. If someone is meant to be in your life, they will rise up to the standards you have set and meet them with respect and grace. For example, if you set a standard that you do not take calls after 11PM, and someone calls after 11, you should make sure the call goes unanswered. This is not rude or controlling. This is how you exercise self-respect. And when you exercise self-respect, that standard will resonate with others. If you have a standard of living within your means, then you must pay your bills before you go shopping. You may have your eye on a new bag or pair of shoes, but failing to uphold an important standard will only add more stress to your life. Consciously causing yourself stress goes against the standards you established for yourself, standards that contribute to maintaining self-love. If you have a standard that the friends in your life must pour as much into you as you pour into them, you will see how the number of your friends drastically change. Some may be willing to happily uphold those standards whereas others will not. React and adjust accordingly.

Having a solid VIP section in your life will raise your standards because they will see what you can be and remind you to stretch further than where you started. Standards are more than boundaries and limitations within relationships. Standards span across various parts of your life – professional, personal, financial, and emotional. You will have a standard for yourself, the way you keep your home, the way people interact with you, and so forth. Many people do not maintain standards out of fear that others will be disappointed or refuse to stick around. This is a critical area for relationships. Many women remain in unhappy relationships, or are mistreated, due to fear – the fear of being alone or fear of further disappointment. The fact of the matter is, if people choose to not keep your standards, they should not be allowed to stay. If anyone is bold enough to openly refuse the standards you have established for yourself, you must be equally bold in refuting those people from muddling around in your life. My husband and I had been dating for about one year when we conceived our first child. I was going to be a mother again. I made up my mind that this time was going to be different. I had an open, honest conversation with him, letting him know I had expectations of being a wife. I would now be a mother of two children, and I deserved and wanted to be a wife. I was sure about what I wanted and transparently expressed my feelings. No longer would I envision a marital fantasy and hope it would come true. I did not have to go back and repeat myself because I knew what I was going to do, whether he proposed or not. You do not have to beg anyone to respect the standards you set.

I was happily engaged a few months later.

If you do not keep standards for yourself, your life will quickly reflect disarray. Your health will be a mess and your mindset will be cluttered. Become serious about your life – say what you mean and mean what you say. When you have standards, and you steadily uphold them, you will see your confidence grow tremendously because you are walking in who God intended you to be – a strong, confident woman. As I grew older and began to forgive myself for my mistakes, I was then determined to establish quality standards for myself – standards that reflect a woman acting out of self-love. I stopped the detrimental habits of my past. No longer would I allow a need for attention to allow myself to be taken advantage of. No more smoking and excessive drinking. No more toxic relationships. I only allow people in my life that love and cherish me. When it comes to my self-worth, I do not allow anyone to have the responsibility of making me feel whole. That is the role God wants to have in your life, and He does not want to share that job with anyone.

Our God is a selfish God, meaning He is not in the business of sharing your attention – He wants your heart to be free to express His goodness, but you must hear His voice. In order to hear His voice, and truly listen, you must walk away from the toxic distractions in your life. Trust that He will gently guide you. After all, He wants you to have a life rich in love – self-love, especially. He wants to be deeply embedded in your spirit so that you speak words of goodness, love, and kindness. As a result, your life will drastically change, and you will become a symbol of hope for others, too.

Today, I am a women's ministry leader, encouraging woman to be all that God called them to be. Sometimes, I cannot believe how my life has transformed, once I established standards and stuck to them. The same young woman who was out of control and did not care about herself has been fully restored and renewed. I am an example that no matter your past, God can still use you to do mighty things. Do not let your lack of standards keep you stuck in the mentality that you are only capable of mediocrity. As long as you have breath, you can set new standards. You decide who you are, not your past and not what you did 10 years ago or even 10 minutes ago. Set your standards and set them high!

Try It on for Size

Make a list of standards you would have if you were the dream woman you have envisioned yourself to be. What would she do on a daily basis? What would she allow and what would she not allow? How does she care for herself and her household? How would your current relationships change, if at all? Once you have created your list, begin implementing the answers in your life. Be honest with where you are, currently. Honesty is of the upmost importance. Practice *being her until you are her!*

Mirror Work

I have set the following standards for myself (*speak out your list*). I am accountable to hold true to the standards I have set. My confidence is dependent on being who I say I am. I am a woman of high standards. Anyone who would like to be in my life must rise to the standards I have set. I am secure. I know who I am.

7 – ARE YOU A MAZDA OR A MASERATI?

"Your value is not given to you. You create it."

What is the difference between a Mazda and a Maserati? Both are cars, getting you from Point A to Point B. The differences are that one vehicle has less value than the other, and one vehicle has more bells and whistles, too. When discussing value, when is the last time you assessed your worth?

A Mazda and a Maserati are treated differently because of the way each car makes a person feel, among other reasons. One is a luxury vehicle and the other is a mid-priced car, making each a completely different driving experience. In comparing a luxury vehicle to a commonplace vehicle, and how those cars make each driver feel, how do you make people feel when they are around you? Do you make others feel as though they are in the presence of luxury? Do you feel luxurious to begin with? These are good questions to explore.

Remember, no one can give you your value. God already said you are valuable and worthy. You belong to Jesus Christ! "You were bought with a price; do not become slaves of men" (1 Corinthians 7:23).

What does a person receive when they are in your presence?

Do they receive a trustworthy friend?

Does your employer receive a determined overachiever?

Do the people you serve receive a true and pure heart?

Are you able to organize, cook, market, design, invent, bake, and create? The list goes on and on.

What God-given talents and abilities do you have to offer to the world?

These are factors that add to your value. The owners of Maserati did not ask anyone how much they think their product is worth. They did not lower the price out of fear others would not want to buy it. They did not halt production because they were worried their car was "too much" for anyone. Instead, they knew the feeling their car would bring to consumers. They knew the specialized options and unique features their product would have, and they set its value accordingly. They knew the type of customers that would be able to afford their car. Consequently, the creators did not lower the value to garner more customers.

That is why a Maserati is considered luxury! Those who can afford this vehicle, do. Those who cannot, admire. The same should go for you – set your value, and do not lower your value for anyone. Do not fear your value will drive anyone away. Those who are driven away were not meant to be in your life. You do not have to make yourself easily assessable in hopes of finding the right person to appreciate you. A keen customer knows value when they see it.

You have to know your value in order to be the type of woman you want be. You will never see a luxury car dealership put one of their cars on clearance, and a luxury car dealership will not make flashy, enticing commercials to lure customers. Instead, they patiently wait on the right buyer. So why would you put yourself on clearance when you know what you have to offer? God gave His son for you! The cross proves your value, so why would you live and think as though you are anything less than worthy?

Stop looking for quantity and start looking for quality relationships.

Stop placing your gifts and talents on the clearance rack.

Stop wearing yourself out trying to convince others you are worthy.

You need to become more choosey of who is in your space, not the other way around.

Earlier in my life, my personal value was hard for me to discover and assess because I was basing my worth on the wrong factors. In short, I established my value on the approval of others.

When I made outstanding grades, those marks earned the approval of my parents and teachers. I was an attractive young lady, so my looks got me attention from boys. I was lacking, though, because that attention never lasted. My value, back then, was based on performance and physicality, two factors which certainly do not determine worth. When I performed well in school or in extracurricular activities, I was applauded, acknowledged, and appreciated. However, when I became a single, teenage mother, the approval I was accustomed to went out of the window. I found myself in a place of desperation for the validation of other people. I believed if I was able to keep their attention then that would make me special, not realizing I was already special without their approval. I now know having a baby at a young age disappointed my parents because they placed a value on me as well. At the time, I was deeply hurt and confused by not meeting the standards they had for me. Instead of finding my value, I used the temporary affection from other people to fill that void. The fairy tale I clung to, and sacrificed so much for, came crashing down and I had no one to fill my desire for approval. This gaping void only intensified my hunt for approval and attention. I put myself in situations I should have never been in, especially with men. I gave myself to people who did not want anything more than a good time. Earning that coveted affection I wanted so badly gave me the exact opposite feeling of what I was hoping for – I valued myself less.

I sadly wondered, "Who have you become? Why are you

doing this, Monique?"

Do not sacrifice your value for company.

After experiencing hurt and embarrassment, more times than I could count, and living in a way that was the total opposite of what I was taught, I had a meeting with myself. Enough was enough. I reached a breaking point. I could either continue on the path of self-destruction or I could veer down the path of attaining self-love. I reminded myself of what I had to offer, and my list was lengthy! I was stronger than I thought, and by having a daughter, I had an obligation to be the best woman I could be, for her and me.

I did not want to put myself on a discounted rate.

I did not want to lower my price to pull people in.

I did not want to make poor decisions in order to prove my worth.

I wanted to be a great example to my child.

I wanted to break the destructive cycle I created.

I could not teach my daughter to value herself if I did not value myself. At that time, I decided to call off the idea of entering new relationships, and, instead, focus on me and my child. I made the decision, once and for all, that if people would not value me, I would willingly and happily be alone. I still hold true to this standard. I will not allow my value to be put on sale. I know no other approval is needed! Not only is approval not needed, but the approval of others is no longer wanted, either, which fills me with an indescribable strength I am able to pass on to my children, too.

During that time of self-reflection, standard setting, and relationship isolation, I realized I could be and should be a better woman. Ironically, during that time, I met my husband. God is the master orchestrator, isn't He? When we stop searching and seeking, we are often gifted new opportunities and relationships. I was working at a local gas station at the time, and in walked the kindest guy I ever met. He was different. He did not come on strong like the guys I was used to. He was polite and gentle. One of my fondest memories of my husband, then boyfriend, is when he used to sit outside of my job at night to make sure I was not alone. He wanted to make sure I was safe. While some people are on guard for controlling reasons, or selfish reasons, my then-boyfriend simply wanted to make sure I was safe during unpredictable, late-night hours. He was, and is, a true gentleman. I was able to appreciate who he was, and learn more about him, because I was not in a desperate space this time around. I was not yearning for attention or begging to be loved. We would sit in his car in front of my mother's apartment and talk for hours. I shared all that I had been through, and he did the same. We talked about our hurts, experiences, goals, and dreams. Having a growing relationship with him was effortless. I did not have to give him anything more than my time. I was growing stronger, and he could see that, too. For another person to acknowledge my growth was the best compliment I could have received at that time. I wanted better for myself. My value was increasing within, and not because of the approval from this man, but because I assessed my value and stuck to my standards.

When you raise your standards and your value, you begin to attract those who can reciprocate what you want and deserve. My husband and I have been married for 11 incredible years and have seven beautiful daughters together. We made the choice to grow together. We committed to working through the challenges marriage inevitably brings. We decided to love, learn, and grow together. I urge you, when you are ready to be in a relationship, to seek out someone who sees the value in you as much or more than you see in yourself. He has been my constant source of love and strength, never judging my past but lifting me up to who I was meant to be, no matter what. *That* is the fairytale I was hoping for. I love you, Derrell. Thank you for not only knowing my worth, but upholding my value and encouraging me to do the same for myself.

Drawing back to the car comparison, and understanding the grave importance of value, another difference between the two cars is how they are treated. You do not park a Maserati just anywhere. You do not resort to parking on a curb or squeezing between two other vehicles in a crowded parking lot. Instead, you put this special car in a garage or have it valeted while out and about.

Furthermore, you do not put any type of gas in the tank. This car only runs smoothly on premium gas. You treat this car with exceptional care because this vehicle is undoubtedly valuable. Consequently, do not treat yourself any random way. Do not fill yourself up with regular gas, meaning, do not allow superficial, temporary appeasement to determine your worth. You are a premium lady and you deserve the best that life has to offer, not only from other people but from yourself. Cherish your body and your mind, you only get one!

Do not treat your body like a rag doll. Treat your body like precious porcelain. Is your body filled with junk like the trunk of a broken down car? Are you using cheap hair products that are drying your hair? Are you using dirty makeup brushes? Would you take your Maserati to a drive-through car wash and risk the chance of scratching its body? Of course not, so why are you washing your face with harsh washes, eating poorly, or allowing someone to abuse you? If you find yourself in an abusive or toxic relationship, get out! You are far too valuable to be treated with anything but the utmost care.

You are not a get-from-Point-A-to-Point-B lady. You are a top-of-the-line woman! A scratch and ding here and there may not seem detrimental to a car, but after a while, those scratches and dings ruin your vehicle the same way unworthy people will scratch and ding you to misery. Put extra time and effort into yourself because you are worthy and valuable, and the sooner you recognize your value, the more confident you will feel!

Try It on for Size

Ask the people closest to you, your VIP's – "What value do I bring to your life?" This exercise will help you understand the depth of what you have to offer. Next, make a list of your talents and abilities. Recognize that you only have as much value as you choose to give yourself. Bounce this list off of your list of standards. Commit to creating the luxury version of yourself.

Mirror Work

My value is not given to me. I create my value. I value myself and choose to live the best version possible. When someone comes in contact with me, I treat them well. I am kind and true. I have so much to offer other people, whether anyone acknowledges my worth or not. I will only allow myself to be in the company of those who value and appreciate my presence and gifts. I am not only valuable, I am a luxury.

8 – TRUTH AND FILTERS

"Comparison is the thief of joy."

In a society overrun with social media presence, we have the ability to let the world see whatever we choose. You can show the world an image or interact with people by typing 140 characters or less. Regardless if your life is going incredibly well or your reality is bleak, social media allows its users to share whatever they want. The majority of people utilize their social media accounts to show their highlight reel, the positive parts of their life.

Do not be deceived, social media is an illusion. While those highlight reel moments are real, no one's life is a perpetual highlight tape. You cannot base your self-worth off of the controlled Internet content. It is so easy to get wrapped up in the number of likes or followers. Do not base your worth off of how other people interact with you via the Internet. I encourage you not to compare yourself to others based on their social media presence. Many of us are envious of people based solely on their planned content, but you cannot see behind the scenes of each person's page. You cannot see the stretch marks under a woman's clothing that make her feel insecure or the negative bank accounts that have a person wildly stressed out. Instead, photos are filtered to give the impression of a picture-perfect life.

Social media comparisons lead to jealousy, especially regarding relationships that may not even exist. We become invested and, at times, consumed, by what we see, when there is no guarantee those images are reality. As a confident woman, you know that it really does not matter, one way or the other, what someone else has because you love your own life! Your life may not be picture-perfect, but you are grateful for the highs, lows, and every moment in between. A father of grateful children will always give his kids more. As God is our Father, He expects us to be grateful for what we have before He will bless us with more. Make a list of everything you are grateful for. You will find that you have more to be thankful for compared to what you feel upset about. As you look over that list, you will see that the life you have is amazing, and when you love your life, you can live your best life! Your confidence in who you are and what you have will stop the need to compete.

You must be able to use social media as entertainment and

not as a means to measure your worth. Comparison is the thief of joy. You cannot be happy when you are comparing yourself to anyone else. There will always be someone smarter, taller, prettier, and wealthier. That is where knowing your value comes into play. You must be sure of who you are and feel grateful for your own life.

The problem with comparing yourself to others is that you forget to study yourself! As I ventured into becoming a confidence coach and speaker, I found myself drawn to the big names I saw on social media. I would admire their events and mass followers. Then, I would circle back to my own platform and see that I had not yet arrived. I began to really study from a place of awe instead of inspiration, and it took a toll. I began to question whether I should make my social media pages more like theirs. The truth is, I have been swept up, from time to time, with social media. That is why I say that being the confident woman you always wanted to be takes constant dedication and a willingness to continually change. I had to take time to remember that who I am is good enough. Who I am meant to touch is going to come from me being me. My worth is not based on followers. My worth is based on the love and purpose I have. Your self-worth is found in the truth of who you are and not the filters you use. Just like the social media sites have filters, so do we. We use filters to mask our imperfections or enhance a picture because we believe that people would like the filtered version far better. Filters can be a good thing, actually. If you want to enhance a beautiful scenic shot, that is understandable, but when you alter your pictures out of fear of what others may think, it becomes too much. If you find yourself truly upset that your posts are not receiving "likes" or "hearts", I want you to reevaluate why you are in need of validation from strangers. Social media is a slippery slope. Watch your step!

If you find yourself experiencing feelings of jealousy towards anyone online, take this piece of advice – remember to take into account that you do not know what that person had to do to get what they have. You may see a woman who has a perfect marriage, a huge home, and gorgeous children, not knowing she may have forced her husband to smile in the picture, their house is a gift from her parents, and her children are driving her crazy. Not that everyone who posts good moments of their lives are not honest, but know that we all want to show our best to our online audience. Do not allow these posts to make you feel as though you are not living up to who you should be. You are meant to have your life, your body, your family, and no one else's. You may want to be someone else, only to discover that if you lived a day in their shoes you would want to give their life back as soon as possible.

Are you filtering your life?

Do you post your messy bedroom and your morning hair?

I would hope not, but you typically don't and neither does anyone else. You can admire or draw inspiration from the people and friends you see online, but do not allow social media, or someone's highlight reel, to overtake your life, or worse, determine your value. Likes online do not equate to self-love! The "like" you should be most concerned about is liking yourself. Double tap into who you are!

Nothing fills our spirits with more bitterness and dissatisfaction than ungratefulness. Having a genuine spirit of gratitude will quickly transform your soul, leading you to contentment and peace. Pull yourself away from the comparison trap, and, instead, thank Him. Thank Him for what you have and do not dwell on what another person has more of. Do you want to be miserable with an empty space in your heart? Of course not! Learn to be grateful, train your mind to steer clear of the comparison trap, and express appreciation every chance you get.

Try It on for Size

Take a good, hard look over your social media presence. What have you been posting and what are the motives behind your posts? Have you been looking for attention? Are you in competition with anyone? How do you feel after assessing your posts? Discouraged? Jealous? Empowered? Be honest with yourself. If you are not pleased with what you discover, choose otherwise. Choose honestly. The truth will set you free.

Mirror Work

My social media is not the means by which I measure my worth. I use different social platforms for entertainment, to connect with family and friends, and gain inspiration. Social media is not a space to vent or gain attention. I am confident in who I am. I do not compare myself to others. I am not fooled by the filters. I am sure of who I am and the woman I know I can continue growing to be.

9 – PEOPLE PLEASING

"When you say 'yes' to everyone, you are saying 'no' to yourself."

My grandfather told me a story that stuck with me for many years. I am not sure where he got this story from, but this tale will help you care less of what people think of you.

> The Old Man, His Son, and the Donkey
> There once was an old man, his son, and a donkey. They were making a journey – the old man walked alongside the donkey, packed down with luggage, and the young son was riding on the donkey. As they trav-

eled along their way, a group of onlookers began to murmur. "Why is this old man walking while his son rides on the donkey? He is old, the son is young. He should be walking." So, the old man said, "Okay, son. You get down and allow me to ride." They continued on their journey and came across another group of people. This group began to ask, "Why is that old man riding and having that poor young man walk? That's not right!" So, the old man thought about it and told his son, "Hey, son, let's both ride on the donkey." So, they went a little farther, and a big crowd began to yell out, "That poor donkey! He is loaded down with that young boy, that old man, and all that luggage. That is just not right!" The old man began to think really hard, and he told the son, "I walked, they complained. You walked, they complained. We both rode, and they complained. So, I have the perfect answer and no one will complain this time... Let's carry the donkey!"

The moral of this story?

No matter what you do, what you think, or how you live your life, someone will always have something to say. Someone will always have an opinion. Some may like the choices you make, others may love them, and there will be those who hate them. No matter which category a person falls in, your life is yours to live, period. Your decisions are yours to believe in, not at the mercy of others to endorse. Set your mind on what you will do with the life you are given and stick with it. Set standards for yourself and stick with them, even when people do not like your decisions or do not understand your choices.

When your self-esteem is dependent on the approval of others, they will be happy and you will be miserable. If you live for their applause, you will die from their disapproval. People are fickle. What they want from you today may be totally different tomorrow. So, does that mean you will continue to change yourself, altering your decisions and feelings, to appease their wants? Absolutely not! You must be secure enough to disappoint people with your choices. It takes a strong person to stand their ground.

If you want to change, make sure you are changing because of your own personal decisions. As human beings, we are constantly renewing our minds, but if you seek to be like the world around you, you will find yourself faced with frustration and disappointment. After all, the desire to be like someone else or the desire to appease someone else is a temporary, fleshly desire that will move you further away from your true purpose, calling, and identity. As I became a leader in women's ministry, I faced several choices. Would I try to be like everyone else who was teaching? Would I try to fashion my messages like the others? Well, I didn't, I did not copy others. I walked my own path, which received quite a bit of push back. Many nights I went home defeated, but God is faithful because there were people continually encouraging me to keep going. I received many calls from people thanking me for helping them in a special, profound way. I had to be me, and remain me, because those who God meant for me to connect with, connected to the real me and not a watered down version of someone else. I did not let the naysayers mold me into someone I was not. I took hold of who I am and embraced my own style of teaching. I encourage you to feel comfortable in your skin, have the confidence to stand your ground, and keep your heart with all diligence (Proverbs 4:23).

My goal is to empower you to use one word, one of the most powerful words in the history of language – NO! Saying "yes" to everyone is saying "no" to yourself, and saying "yes" will make them happy while leaving you drained. As you go through this self-progression journey, setting boundaries and standards, do not expect everyone to be excited about your growth. Growth scares others. Insecure people are uncomfortable when they witness others growing and progressing because they have yet to grow and progress.

Some may say you are conceited or that you have changed. Those are signs that they either do not know who they are or they are upset that they are not getting their way! You cannot be afraid to stand in your truth. The need to please can overtake you because you get a temporary fix from the attention.

The need to please others mirrors a similar reaction to

gambling. You pull the lever of the slot machine and sometimes you hit the jackpot and sometimes you don't. The problem is that you have to pay every time you pull. Similarly, we think that if we never say "no" we will get the reward of appreciation and praise. *Wrong*. You will get taken advantage of if you live your life for others. If the people in your life know they can guilt you, or that you do not have set boundaries, they will take and take. Your need for their approval will drive you past what you know you are un-willing to do. This will create a perpetual cycle of being used and feeling disappointed. You are supposed to help others. Service is a sign of a loving, sound person, but make sure the motives are coming from the right place. Sadly, some folks serve others for their own benefit. Be discerning but not doubtful.

Are you always saying "yes" because your willingness to help is from your heart or because you are afraid others will be upset if you say "no"?

Do have more positions in ministry than you can handle?

Do you always pick up that one friend, even when you don't feel like it?

Do you regularly loan money to others, even when your bank account is low?

Are you putting everyone's needs before your own?

Are you sacrificing too much of yourself for others?

Will the same people you are jumping over oceans for jump a puddle for you?

The people in your life who are meant to remain will understand that you may not do everything they want. Furthermore, you should not expect them to do everything you ask. A confident woman is not a people pleaser. She is secure in her "yes" and assertive in her "no".

Do you remember the donkey story at the beginning of the chapter? Keep in mind – someone will always be there to criticize or discourage you when you decide to stand firm in your choices and decisions. Be strong!

Try It on for Size

Look over your current calendar. Are there events you committed to that you do not want to attend? Do you have weeks filled with obligations and social events with your church or your loved ones? Decide which does and does not give you joy. Make a conscious decision to remove what you do not want to be doing. Make sure you have not been saying "yes" out of fear you may be disappointing someone. Practice saying "no" in the mirror until you feel comfortable saying this word with confidence.

Mirror Work

I am not a hostage to the words or requests of others. If I say "no", that does not make me a bad person. I will say "yes" to the people I love and the tasks that are priorities in my life. I will say "no" to the things that will not push me forward or that I do not want to do. I am secure in who I am. I mean what I say and I say what I mean.

10 – WALK IT OUT

"It's not the person with the most knowledge that is the most powerful. It is the one who uses the knowledge."

The last few chapters have covered several tips and steps towards being the confident woman you have always wanted to be. If you want to convert your list of ideals to a real, lasting transformation, you must apply what you learned and accomplished from the exercise and affirmation sections! You have to put that little black dress of confidence on and rock it!

So, how do you walk it out?

You walk out into the world as the woman you want to be. You are not becoming her. *You are her!* Through each exercise, you have been given a practical step towards building your confidence. Your affirmations allow you to hear yourself telling you who you are, the true you, the confident you!

Let's recap on your progress and accomplishments...

Through the above-listed exercises and affirmations, you have created a woman with an open heart capable of genuine forgiveness. You are no longer hostage to your pain or your past. You have willingly let yourself off the hook, and you are proud of who you are, flaws and all. You have created a secure woman who is grounded in faith by seeing yourself as God sees you. You can now see yourself through the eyes of the One who made you, and He thinks you are awesome!

You are now a more attractive and secure woman through what you have learned in *Mirror, Mirror*. You are also a woman of her word. You are aware of the words you speak and how they will affect your life and the lives of others. You have become a master of your words because you know their power.

You have solid friendships, and you are a wonderful friend in return. You are clear on where each person stands in your life. You have taken back your power to choose the people in your life, and you have a specific expectation on how you are to be treated. You are a woman who has standards, high standards. You expect nothing less than the best, and you will not tolerate anything less, either. You know your value, and you are secure in what you can do and what you can offer to the world. You know you deserve to be treated like luxury because you are luxury!

No longer do you look for validation through social media.

You are secure and content with the life you have, and you do not compare yourself to other women. You have a clear, unfiltered picture of who you are. Most of all, you are comfortable with the truth of who you are.

What do you do if you find yourself slipping back into old patterns? As I shared before, I have experienced several bouts of regression. You do not just let yourself revert all the way back to your old ways. The journey is not about being perfect. The journey is about being in a state of constant evolution.

If you have a rough day and use negative words, correct your train of thought.

If you find yourself in a relationship that is not up to your standards, adjust.

When you realize a current friendship is not going in the direction you want it to, choose your next step wisely.

This mode of thinking, despite regression, will propel you closer to the self-confident woman you want to be. This mentality must become part of your day-to-day life. You are a confident woman, so you are required to live fully! No one will make you remain confident or hold your hand on your personal journey. You have to make a decision as to whether or not you want to be a perpetually confident woman, overflowing with self-love. If are your finally tired of being who you have been, yet determined to be the woman you know you can be, you get back up, dust yourself off, and go about life differently, but this time for the best!

I have used the principles in this book to begin to live my

best life. I am far from the insecure and attention-seeking teen I was many years ago. I have allowed Christ to make a change in me, and He has rewarded me with a leadership position, a role of helping women realize they are never too far for God to reach them. He has given me the know-how and assurance to reach women all over the world, especially through this book. My greatest blessing, though, is my seven beautiful daughters. He has entrusted me to instill these self-reliant, poised principles in each of them. I am able to juggle the roles of wife, mother, speaker, leader, and now, author, by deciding to live in my truth and not compromise my reality for anyone. My confidence is whole and complete because I know who I am and what I have to give to this world. I believe that you, too, can live the life of your dreams by releasing your past, replacing your former habits with improved practices, and moving on to thrive in any area of your life that you so choose. You have all the tools to succeed, you just have to choose to walk it out!

Congratulations, you did it! You have made it to the runway of life, and the world is waiting to see you strut. Just like your little black dress, your self-esteem is what you must wear with pride. You are the woman you always wanted to be, you just had to pull her out of the back of your closet. I pray you have found something in these pages that you may have not thought of before, and I pray that you choose to implement those lessons into your daily life. The world is waiting for you to become the confident woman you have always wanted to be. I want to thank you for allowing me to share my story and offer guidance along the way.

Final Mirror Work

I not only take in information, but I apply information to my life. I take my confidence seriously. I choose the life I want to have. I am in control of my emotions, and I am the confident woman I have always wanted to be. I will work on myself, daily, to become more and more of who God has called me to be. I am not a slave to my pain. I am whole, I am secure. My self-esteem is one of my life essentials, and just like my little black dress, my self-esteem is never going out of style.

ABOUT THE AUTHOR

Monique Mays is an inspirational speaker, teacher, women's ministry leader, and author. Her many years in women's ministry birthed a profound passion to empower and encourage women to love God and themselves. She is also the founder and CEO of MM Confidence Coaching. Her motto is *Release, Renew, and Thrive*. By giving women the tools to release the chains of their past, renew their self-esteem, and thrive in the life God has for them, she continues to make an impact among women all over the world.

Monique currently resides in Houston, Texas, with her husband and seven daughters.

For more information visit:
www.moniquemays.com

If you are looking for continued support through your journey, visit my social media sites:
Facebook: www.facebook.com/mmyourconfidencecoach
Instagram: @m.m_yourconfidencecoach

www.ingramcontent.com/pod-product-compliance
Lightning Source LLC
Chambersburg PA
CBHW072153090426
42740CB00012B/2248